The God
of Chance *and* Purpose

The God of Chance and Purpose

Divine Involvement in a Secular Evolutionary World

BRADFORD McCALL

Foreword by John F. Haught

WIPF & STOCK · Eugene, Oregon

THE GOD OF CHANCE AND PURPOSE
Divine Involvement in a Secular Evolutionary World

Copyright © 2022 Bradford McCall. All rights reserved. Except for brief quotations in critical publications or reviews, no part of this book may be reproduced in any manner without prior written permission from the publisher. Write: Permissions, Wipf and Stock Publishers, 199 W. 8th Ave., Suite 3, Eugene, OR 97401.

Wipf & Stock
An Imprint of Wipf and Stock Publishers
199 W. 8th Ave., Suite 3
Eugene, OR 97401

www.wipfandstock.com

PAPERBACK ISBN: 978-1-7252-8383-1
HARDCOVER ISBN: 978-1-7252-8384-8
EBOOK ISBN: 978-1-7252-8385-5

01/20/22

Contents

Dedication   vii
Foreword by John F. Haught   ix
Acknowledgments   xi

Introduction: Divine Involvement in a Secular Evolutionary World   xiii
1   A Tripartite Contemporary Relation of Science & Theology   1

Part I | Preliminary Considerations—The Secular Evolutionary Worldview (SEW)

2   The Secular Evolutionary Worldview (SEW) Defined & Explicated   19
3   The God of Chance: An Elucidation of Chance in (Macro-)Evolution   59

Part II | The God of Chance and Purpose—Theological Assists by Philip Clayton and Alister McGrath

4   The God of Contemporary Science: Dialoguing with Clayton   93
5   A (Renewed) Natural Theology: Dialoguing with McGrath   102
6   Conclusion: A New Natural Theology from Below— An Affirmation of Ontological Randomness and Purpose in Nature   115

Bibliography   125

Dedication

For years prior to my meeting of Dr. Amos Yong, I had somewhat curiously—either intentionally or unintentionally—run *away* from my biological past that included both an undergraduate degree from the university system of Georgia as well as a several years of full-time work done thereafter as a research associate at Emergent Genetics, Inc., making things that God did not. Indeed, after my (dramatic) conversion to Christianity in a cotton field located in Vienna, Georgia (off Highway 27 West, about one and a half miles outside of the city limits, on the eastern-most side of the road, at circa 1:12 p.m. . . .) on the twenty-fourth of July, 2000, I immersed myself in strict biblical studies. In fact, I purged myself of all of my library holdings related to biology. I went through, one might say, a forceful purgation of my past. I wallowed in disarray, however, bifurcating what I knew to be true from my prior biological undertakings from what I then—in a growing fashion—thought to be true about God.

I even began preaching the faith that I once detested so heavily about a year and a half after my conversion experience. During my initial seminary years, from 2001 to 2003, not much thought was given to my biological heritage. In fact, I first went to New Orleans Baptist Theological Seminary, and gave little to no thought to the processes of (macro-)evolution, as well as all that those processes entail. Then, midcourse, I transferred to Asbury Theological Seminary after

Dedication

I had a "personal encounter," so to speak, with the thought and theology of John Wesley in 2002, and I became convinced that Wesley gave a unique and apropos model with which to formulate my theology. Yet, I still had not recovered my biological past. Still running *from* it, one might say. Indeed, I even got caught up in the intelligent design movement for a short time, which caused me to further relegate my biological past to the proverbial dustbin of my history.

After I attained a preaching position at Fredonia Congregational Methodist Church in Barnesville, Georgia, during the first month of 2006, I thought to myself, Why not explore a PhD in a religiously-oriented program? So I began searching, and hit upon one at Regent University at their Virginia Beach campus. I first met Amos Yong in the summer of 2006, during my first residency in Regent's modular PhD program. My word, was that a life-changing endeavor! Amos was my advisor there, and he (almost) immediately began to both coach and provoke me to resurrect my biological training, and thereafter appropriate it *for* God, not running *away* from it like I had theretofore. He incisively instructed me in another modality of thought, one that did not *neglect* biology, but one that *employed* it instead.

While Amos is no biologist, I actually learned more biology—at least the *philosophy of biology*—while studying under him than I did in my pointed years of biological study in my undergraduate program. Amos taught me that I did not need to fear my biological past, but should embrace it instead. In no small way, all that I have done in the theology and science conversation post-2006 is a direct result of his initial leadership. Additionally, Amos's distinct focus on pneumatology has impacted me to no end and given me a lens through which I see all of reality.

So, it is with these considerations in mind that I dedicate this volume explicitly to Amos Yong—you have impacted my life to an unimaginable degree, and for that I am grossly thankful. I aspire to be half the theologian in the *future* that you are right *now*. I can truly say that I adore that man, not only for what he has done in my life, but also for what that means to me. *By* chance, I met Amos; *for* chance, he introduced me to the thought of Charles Sanders Peirce. And I have not been the same since.

Foreword

WHEN EVOLUTIONISTS GIVE US their understanding of biology, more often than not their science comes wrapped in the ideology of materialism, a belief system that squeezes the juice right out of evolution. Bradford McCall is unusually sensitive to the way in which Darwin's science has been kidnapped by philosophers who present evolution to students, scholars, and the general public as proof of the pointlessness of the universe—and as the last nail in the coffin of religious faith.

The author of this book knows better. He is aware that hidden metaphysical assumptions accompany not only religious but also scientific interpretations of the natural world and that this is especially true of evolution. McCall wants to make sure that we recognize the ideological or metaphysical leanings tacitly shaping allegedly objective interpretations of evolutionary biology. In this thoughtful work, he presents a tidy alternative to such ideologists as the best-selling scientist and author Richard Dawkins who scarcely disguises his usage of Darwinian evolution to support his preference for materialist atheism.

Particularly interesting and controversial in attempts to understand Darwin is how to interpret the meaning of "chance." Chance, along with natural selection and deep time, is taken to be an essential ingredient in nature's rather simple recipe for evolution.

Foreword

But what does "chance" really mean? And has anybody probed fully what it means for our understanding of the cosmos and God?

It is the task of philosophy and theology to address this question. Ever since Darwin the predominant philosophical and theological interpretation of the high degree of accident in nature is that of poet Alexander Pope: "Chance [is] direction which thou canst not see."

Bradford McCall thinks we can do better than this. Chance is not just a signal of the poverty of human minds. It is not just a coverup for a carefully designed universe. Rather it is a reality that keeps the cosmos open to the future and gives it an autonomy that allows us to love it and wait for it to become something more. Taking advantage of the rarely discussed but brilliant philosophical work of Charles Sanders Peirce, McCall offers here a unique interpretation of the role of chance in evolution. In doing so he makes the universe and the story of life much more interesting and more precious than the conventional materialist interpretations of nature will ever allow.

—John F. Haught, Research Professor at Georgetown University, and author of many books related to science, faith, and evolution, including *Resting on the Future: Catholic Theology for an Unfinished Universe* (Bloomsbury, 2015), and *The New Cosmic Story: Inside Our Awakening Universe* (Yale, 2017).

Acknowledgments

I WOULD LIKE TO begin by thanking Philip Clayton, my soon-to-be *Doktor vater*, for taking the time to review this manuscript prior to my submission of it to Wipf & Stock. He prevented numerous mindless errors on my part. Any error that remains, of course, is totally my responsibility. That said, I would also like to offer generous thanks to my mother, Susan R. Brown, without whose financial prowess over the last past quarter-century, I might have had to go out and get a real job. Writing, after all, is not a real job, is it? I would also like to extend hearty thanks to John F. Haught for writing such a stunning Foreword. With friends like him promoting my work, I might never have to work again! While my dedication of this book to Amos Yong speaks for itself, I would like also now to reiterate that he has had a formative influence on me over the last fifteen-some-odd years, and that I am most appreciative of that fact. Finally, I desire to thank the entire faculty at Claremont School of Theology in Claremont, California, for putting up with me the last three years. I know it has been hard. But it was *not* purposeful in this instance, only a matter of *chance* instead.

Introduction

Divine Involvement in a Secular Evolutionary World

An Overview of This Book's Contents

THIS BRIEF TITLE WILL pursue a triangulation of chance, divine involvement, and theology through a fundamentally Peircean lens—at least epistemologically and semiotically. The argument proceeds over five distinct chapters and a conclusion, which constitutes a sixth chapter. In this introduction to the overall argument of the book, I interact principally with the historic dimensions of the Darwinian synthesis within evolutionary biology. I then delineate several aspects of previous models of the relationship between science and theology/religion in chapter 1.

Indeed, within the academy today, there are four general ways of responding to the main question of chapter 1. On the one hand, we have those who think there are no real limits to the competencies of science, what it can do, and what it can explain. An example of this type of thinking is found within the thought of Richard Dawkins. Mikael Stenmark calls people like Dawkins "scientific expansionists." What they have in common is that they think science can and should be *expanded* in such a way that the only kind of knowledge that we can have is of a scientific variety.

Introduction

On the other hand, there are people who contend that science should be heavily informed by or shaped by religion. Stenmark calls these individuals "religious expansionists." There is yet another group of views on the science and theology relationship, one that contends that science cannot be ideologically neutral. Stenmark refers to these thinkers as "ideological expansionists." In contradistinction to the aforementioned three models, there is a fourth group of thinkers that defends the idea that science and theology or ideology ought to be restricted to their own separate areas of inquiry. Stenmark calls these people "scientific and religious restrictionists." Moreover, I suggest a model of the relationship between science and theology that is monistic, is influenced by some process philosophy,[1] and is *overlapping* with respect to these two domains of inquiry.

In chapter 2 of this book, which opens part I, I discuss the Modern Synthetic theory in evolutionary biology. In particular, I refer to what I have labeled the secular evolutionary worldview (SEW). I provide a brief explanation of the SEW, and then address major topics, theses, and sub-theses of the worldview. For example, I note how common ancestry of all animals is revealed by the SEW. Then, I note how the SEW asserts adaptationism as being the driving force of all evolutionary advancement. Further, I explicate natural selection as being the methodology behind adaptationism, which leads to my next point, that is, an overview of natural selection in speciation. I then explain my understanding of the units of selection, whether it be individual or group-based.

In the third chapter of this book, I dismiss the French physicist Pierre-Simon de Laplace's claim that a sufficiently informed intelligence could forecast everything that is going to happen in the whole universe, and, working backwards, could tell you everything that did happen, not by direct citation and rebuke, but rather by implicit argumentation and demonstration of the *God of Chance*. History includes too much contingency, or the shaping of present results by long chains of unpredictable antecedent states, rather than immediate determination, for a position—such as Laplace's—to be

1. As in, I garner elements from process philosophy, but it is not the foundation for my argument in this book.

Introduction

palatable. In this chapter of the book, I argue that ontological randomness is genuine. God does not directly determine the outcome of every scientifically random event, but instead generally constrains randomness by setting broad boundaries. God then allows particles, organisms, and systems to interact according to natural laws within these boundaries, thereby producing a wide range of beautifully complex results. Indeed, I first show this by garnering insights from an influential book entitled *Chance in Evolution*, edited by Grant Ramsey and Charles H. Pence. Thereafter, I discuss insights gleaned from another influential title, *The Challenge of Chance*, edited by Klaas Landsman and Ellen van Wolde, which complement Ramsey and Pence's contentions, mentioned earlier.

Then, in part II of this book, I explore the God of chance and purpose, with theological assists provided by Philip Clayton and Alister McGrath over two chapters (chapters 4 and 5, respectively). So, then, we live in a world of both chance and purpose. One may even go so far as to state that this world is designed for both chance and purpose, though one needs to be wary of allowing overly anthropomorphic notions to creep into the analysis. Rational beings, in this scenario, are not *ipso facto* required for God to constrain randomness, as the degree of influence the deity has is dependent upon the level of sentience that the entity possesses.

Four General Phases of Darwinism

What follows is my original conceptioning of historic Darwinism viewed as a whole: Indeed, I contend that there are three general themes concerning historic Darwinism that correspond to three general phases in the evolution of Darwinism. Each of these themes may be thought of as corresponding to a phase in the evolution of Darwinism. The first such phase corresponds to the period from the publication of *On the Origin of Species* in 1859 to the first quarter of the twentieth century. Although there had been positions put forth regarding the various evolutionary theories and the competing debates about those evolutionary theories before *On the Origin of Species*, it was Darwin's work that succeeded in convincing both

Introduction

the scientific community and the wider public of the fact that all species are related to one another.[2] Darwin's phrase "descent with modification," though he preferred to the term "evolution," sums up clearly the concept of evolutionary continuity. This first phase of Darwinism is marked by the importance of natural selection as an explanation of evolutionary change.

This first phase of Darwinism came to fruition in the late 1920s and early 1930s, during which the importance of natural selection as an explanation of evolutionary change was confirmed, following from the synthesis of natural selection with Gregor Mendel's rediscovered theory of particulate inheritance based on his experimental genetics work with pea plants, which was originally conducted at a near contemporaneous time as Darwin's theorizing and which was then wedded with Darwinism. This coupling led it to be termed the "neo-Darwinian" synthesis, which led, logically, to the second general phase of Darwinism. So, then, phase two refers to the period of time between the 1930s to 1972. Within this period, there was a marked emphasis placed upon *particulate inheritance*: this is the phase of Darwinism in which Mendel's genetics work was expanded by various thinkers to all facets of Darwinism, which was, for all intents and purposes, the paradigm of Darwinism.

Phase three was marked by an over-emphasis upon *contingency*. This period of time was sparked by a publication in 1972 that shell-shocked neo-Darwinism. Indeed, this period or phase arose after the publication of a seminal paper by Stephen Jay Gould and Niles Eldredge entitled "Punctuated Equilibria: The Tempo and Mode of Evolution Reconsidered," wherein they argue that evolution is marked by long periods of stasis, after which rapid (geologically speaking) advancements of complexity occur, which is in contradistinction to the gradualism of historic Darwinism. Moreover, this theory avers that contingency is the primal aspect of evolution, not natural selection; that is, if the tape of life were to be re-run, the specific outcomes—and even the broad outlines—of evolution would be drastically different: we would not get anything like the same thing(s) or entities twice.

2. Brooke, *Science and Religion*, 226–74.

Introduction

This third phase in the history of Darwinism may be thought of as originating in the 1970s with various pressures on the neo-Darwinian synthesis.[3] A feature common to the consequent expansions of the neo-Darwinian synthesis is the theme of contingency. As Depew and Weber say of current evolutionary biology:

> Just as Darwin's work exploded the Victorians' cozy sense of space and time, so contemporary evolutionary speculation is forcing twentieth-century Darwinians to adjust to the even more expansive, chancy, contingent worldview that is already present in modern cosmology but that has so far been contained in evolutionary biology by the comforting rationalism of our talk about adaptations, according to which, even if we do not invoke God, we still seem to be able to give good reasons for what we see around us.[4]

Into this modern retrieval of the import of chance in evolutionary explanations, I would like to propose a *fourth* general phase of Darwinian evolution: *correlationism*, wherein Peirce's evolutionary developmental teleology, which I will roughly outline in this title, is a mediating third way between total chance on one side and total determination on the other. The operation of chance, however, shows an uncanny tendency to bring about unlikely events by various means under varying circumstances. I will be working toward this fourth general phase not only by the contents of this book, but also by other contracted books to come out in future years. Having said all of the above, let us now step into the "meat" of this book.

---

3. Depew and Weber, *Evolution at a Crossroads*, 14.
4. Depew and Weber, *Evolution at a Crossroads*, 15.

1

A Tripartite Contemporary Relation of Science & Theology

IMPRESSED BY WILLIAM PALEY's logic and eye for detail, the young Charles Darwin accepted the conventional observation that organisms were adapted exquisitely to their environments. This remarkable fact, Darwin agreed at the time, could only be explained by reference to the existence of an intelligent and benign creator.[1] Having overcome the initial objections of his father, Robert, Charles accepted Capitan Fitzroy's offer to be his gentlemanly companion on an exploration of various unknown lands, setting sail in 1831 on what would turn out to be an endlessly fascinating five-year voyage around the globe on the *Beagle*. It was a journey that would give surprising new direction to Darwin's own life and also provide information about nature that has agitated the religious sensibilities of many theists ever since.

After returning home, Darwin's earlier belief in the special creation of each distinct species transmutated into a strong suspicion that the origin of different living species had occurred gradually, in a purely natural way. Among the many questions that Darwin and

1. Haught, *Making Sense of Evolution*, 6.

other naturalists who thereafter studied the specimens he collected on the *Beagle* voyage began to ask was, Why do small but distinct variations appear among geographically distributed species of birds and other animals? Specific differences in species, Darwin began to suppose, could be accounted for without divine special creation if there had been minute, cumulative changes in living organisms over an immensely long time. In fact, following his return from the voyage of the Beagle, Darwin wrote of his own views,

> The old argument from design in nature, as given by Paley, which formerly seemed to me so conclusive, fails, now that the law of natural selection has been discovered. There seems to be no more design in the variability of organic beings and in the action of natural selection, than in the course which the wind blows.[2]

In offering the mechanism of natural selection, Darwin gave a new kind of answer to what had previously been viewed as a strictly theological question. After he published his theory in 1859, Darwin effectively made natural science the new kind of ultimate explanation by making science itself able to provide a new answer to a very old theological question. After all, if natural science can account for something as complex as living organisms, including things as seemingly simple as the fish's eye and eventually as complex as even the human brain, had not science then taken over theology's place in the task of making life's apparent designs fully intelligible? If natural selection is the ultimate cause of apparent design, do classic theological explanations matter at all? What good is theology if science can provide a satisfying answer to one of humanity's most burning questions?[3] These questions are still quite alive today—over one hundred and fifty years later.

Notably, in the wake of the *On the Origin of Species*, religion underwent a significant reformulation. God, who had previously been seen as the primary artist of nature, began to be viewed as a more distant deity—even more so than the developments of Newton in the previous century had relegated him. Responses to the theory

2. Darwin, *Autobiography*.
3. Haught, *Making Sense of Evolution*, 13.

A Tripartite Contemporary Relation of Science & Theology

of evolution by religious communities proceeded along several lines, from outright rejection by the fundamentalists to cautioned acceptance by the religious moderates, to unquestioned acceptance by theological liberals. Fundamentalists viewed Darwinism as an attack on the tenets of Christianity and therefore rejected the insights gleaned from the science of evolution. Scientifically, there were also mixed reactions to the advent of Darwinism, ranging from outright rejection to qualified acceptance to full embrace. Following his famous teacher Georges Cuvier, Louis Agassiz asserted that the major groups of animals do *not* represent ancestral branches of a hypothetical evolutionary tree but, instead, document a great plan that was used by the Creator to design the many different species in existence today. Asa Gray, however, was a Presbyterian Christian scientist who heartily accepted Darwinism. He spent much of his life arguing on both a popular and a scientific level for the compatibility of evolutionary theory and religion by contending that natural selection was not inconsistent with a deity superintending the process of evolution. He gives us a model to follow today.

People throughout the ages have attempted to understand the universe and their place within it. In attempting to develop a worldview that explicates their position in the world, religions have typically played a very important role, but particularly since the biological revolution onset by Darwin, biology has also played a crucial role. How should we attempt to understand the relationship between science and theology/religion? In what follows, I will attempt to answer this overarching question by cursorily examining several attempts in the past to classify the science and theology relationship. I will also develop my personal view of the relation between science and theology, with a heavy reliance upon the concepts of biology.

A Delineation of Models Regarding the Relationship between Science and Theology

In this section of chapter 1, I delineate several aspects of previous models of the relationship between science and theology/religion. John Hedley Brooke and Geoffrey Cantor, for example, argue that neither religion nor science is reducible to some sort of timeless essence; rather, both must be understood in their historical particularities—they are inextricable from the times in which they arise.[4] Within the literature on the science and theology relationship today, there are four general ways of responding to the main question of this chapter. On the one hand, we have those who think that there are no real limits to the competencies of science, what it can do, and what it can explain. Richard Dawkins, for example, writes that since we have modern biology, we have "no longer . . . to resort to superstition when faced with the deep problems: Is there a meaning to life? What are we for? What is man?"[5]

Note also here that the thirty-year debate between Stephen Jay Gould and Dawkins is very contentious in its nature, continuing up to the death of Gould in 2002. Since then, their feud has continued through various proxies. It may be said that Dawkins and Gould agree on much. They are pretty well in line about the basics of the evolutionary advance. Life is over four billion years old. Bacteria were the first life forms. There is no inevitability in evolution. There is no aim or purpose in evolution. The fundamental difference between the two scientists, it may be surmised, is that they represent two different schools of thought within the evolutionary sciences: ethology (Dawkins), and paleontology (Gould). Ethologists focus upon behavior, whereas paleontologists center upon the excavation of and reconstruction of past life, mainly through the fossil record. Paleontologists are, if you will, the "historians" of nature. More fundamental to the dispute between the two biologists, however, in my opinion, is their radically different conceptions of evolutionary biology. For Dawkins, adaptedness—i.e., the "fit" between an organism and its environment—is the primary problem of evolutionary biology.

Dawkins's answer to the derivation of complexity by means of adaptation is Darwinian natural selection. Gould sees the world differently; as a paleontologist, he has a different conception of the mechanism of evolution. Based upon my studies, three differences

4. Brooke and Cantor, *Reconstructing Nature*, ix.
5. Dawkins, *The Selfish Gene*, 1.

A Tripartite Contemporary Relation of Science & Theology

between him and Dawkins stand out, in fact. First, Gould places more emphasis upon the import of chance; second, the influence of genes in evolution is less important for Gould than for Dawkins. And third, selection is also less powerful for Gould than for Dawkins. A fourth distinction could also perhaps be made, but this is more tentatively posited by me: Dawkins's view of biology, it could be said, is more active and variable, whereas Gould's views are relatively more static and less variable. According to Dawkins, science can address and answer all of these questions. Mikael Stenmark calls people like Dawkins "scientific expansionists."[6] What they have in common is that they think science can and should be *expanded* in such a way that the only kind of knowledge that we can have is of a scientific variety.

On the other hand, there are people that contend science should be heavily informed by or even shaped by religion. These thinkers aver that the boundaries of religion—not those of science—can and should be *expanded* in such a way that religion dictates science. Stenmark calls these individuals "religious expansionists."[7] For instance, in this camp one will find such thinkers as Alvin Plantinga, who, while noting that it is naive to expect contemporary science to be religiously or theologically neutral, advises us that it would be wise that "a Christian academic and scientific community ought to pursue science in its own way, starting from and taking for granted what they know as Christians."[8] I contend that we must take religious expansionists as seriously as we take scientific expansionists.

There is yet another group of views on the science and theology relationship, one that contends science cannot be ideologically neutral. Richard Lewontin, Steven Rose, and Leon J. Kamin, for example, are representatives of this view; they write that they "share a commitment to the prospect of the creation of a more socially just—a socialist—society. And we recognize that a critical science

---

6. Stenmark, *How to Relate Science and Religion*, xi. Note that Stenmark gets the terminology of "scientific expansionists" from Graham, who notes that expansionists write in such a way that the boundaries of science "include, at least by implication, value questions," Graham, *Between Science and Values*, 6.

7. Stenmark, *How to Relate Science and Religion*, xii.

8. Plantinga, "Science: Augustinian or Duhemian?," 497.

is an integral part of the struggle to create that society."[9] Stenmark calls these thinkers "ideological expansionists."[10]

In contradistinction to the three above mentioned models, there is a fourth group of thinkers that defends the idea that science and theology or ideology ought to be restricted to their own separate areas of inquiry; Stenmark calls these people "scientific and religious restrictionists."[11] An example of this type of thinking can be found in the writings of Gould, who argues that science and religion should exhibit a respectful noninterference, and are in fact autonomous, "non-overlapping magisteria."[12] The magisterium of science regards the empirical realm, whereas religion regards questions of ultimate meaning and moral value.[13]

Both science and theology have social dimensions, and as such they are social practices, meaning that they are "Socially established cooperative human activities through which their practitioners . . . try to achieve certain goals by means of particular strategies."[14] I agree with Stenmark here. I contend that science and theology have social practices that *overlap*. It is often claimed that science is the paradigm of dispassionate inquiry, where positions of truth are critically examined, and nothing is believed on the basis of authority; instead, the scientific community disinterestedly applies the scientific method. I question this claim, and contend instead, with Kuhn,[15] that all scientific truths are socially constrained. Moreover, since the practice of science is a learned activity, it, like religion, employs the usage of authority. And if one would like to question that claim, attend a scientific conference or two, and that fact will become quite clear. Philip Kitcher agrees, writing, "individual scientists identify certain people within the community

---

9. Lewontin et al., *Not in Our Genes*, ix–x.
10. Stenmark, *How to Relate Science and Religion*, xiii.
11. Stenmark, *How to Relate Science and Religion*, xiv.
12. Gould, *Rocks of Ages*, 5.
13. Gould, *Rocks of Ages*, 6.
14. Stenmark, *How to Relate Science and Religion*, xvi.
15. Cf. Kuhn, *The Structure of Scientific Revolutions*.

as authoritative in issues that are not agreed on throughout the community."[16]

A (Late-)Modern Depiction of Science & Theology as Overlapping

Early in my postgraduate education, I encountered process philosophy, and my life has been forever changed as a result. This section of chapter 1 will briefly recount its continuing relevance for me, and how my advocacy of a monistic process-influenced view of the *overlapping* relationship between science and theology looks like fleshed out in practice. In my studies over the last fifteen years, I have consistently sought to *integrate* my new learning with my undergraduate degree in biology. While I here use the term "integrate," this should not be taken to mean that I indiscriminately agree with Ian Barbour's characterization of what he calls the "integration" position of the science and religion relationship.[17] Due to his highly read book, most of the discussion post-1990 has classified the science and theology relationship as being one of the following: conflict, independence, dialogue, or integration.

Because I view the notion of there being a "conflict" between science and religion as a specious concept, based more so on John William Draper's polemic against the Catholic Church, as expressed in his *History of the Conflict between Religion and Science* (1874), as well as my contention that the putative relation known as "dialogue" is nebulous (regardless of which view one might hold, they should be committed to "dialogue" with opposing views), I would—if I had to use Barbour's delineations—be an integrationist. But overall, I agree with Brooke and Cantor[18] and van Huyssteen,[19] who argue that Barbour's classification scheme is too ahistorical, universal, and static to fruitfully map the way science and religion have interacted. So, then, in what follows, one may find an explication

---

16. Kitcher, *The Advancement of Science*, 84n36.
17. Cf. Barbour, *Religion in an Age of Science*, 77.
18. Brooke and Cantor, *Reconstructing Nature*, 275.
19. van Huyssteen, *Duet or Duel?*, 3.

of how I contend the science and theology relationship should be characterized by a *monistic* understanding of the two domains that is heavily ideologically influenced (i.e., on the process worldview of Whitehead and Hartshorne), and is discernable by an *overlapping* of the two fields of study, or to employ Gould's preferred language, "magisteria."

Process philosophy is based on the conviction that the central task of philosophy is to construct an over-arching cosmology in which all intuitions grounded in human experience can be reconciled. Cosmology is a fundamental science. Biology is a subset of science, and thus related also to cosmology, although I admit that cosmology and evolution involve different aspects of science at large. Nevertheless, whereas cosmologies were traditionally based on religious, ethical, and aesthetic as well as scientific experiences, cosmology in the modern period has increasingly been based on science alone. In the broadest sense, the term "process philosophy" refers to all worldviews holding that process or becoming is more fundamental than unchanging—or static—being.[20] The term has widely come to refer in particular, however, to the movement inaugurated by Whitehead and extended by Hartshorne.

So how does this monistic advocation of a process-influenced view of the overlapping relationship between science and theology actually look? One side of this task of reconciling science and theology involves the replacement of the materialistic worldview, with which science has been associated primarily since the nineteenth century, with "panexperientialism," which allows religious experience to be taken seriously. The term "panexperientialism" was coined in 1977 by American theologian-philosopher David Ray Griffin, and is a combination of the terms *"pan,"* meaning all, and "experience." The theory of panexperientialism is summarized in Griffin's 1998 book *Unsnarling the World-Knot: Consciousness,*

---

20. One can find advocation of these views in an anthology edited by Browning and Myers, entitled *Philosophers of Process*, which includes selections from Samuel Alexander, Henri Bergson, John Dewey, William James, Conway Lloyd Morgan, Charles Sanders Peirce, and Alfred North Whitehead, with an introduction by Charles Hartshorne.

A Tripartite Contemporary Relation of Science & Theology

Freedom, and the Mind-Body Problem,[21] in which he argues that Whitehead advocates a monistic metaphysic; thus, the traditional problems of mind-body interaction are not present in process metaphysics because reality, at its base, is not bifurcated into purely mental or physical categories. This process-metaphysical doctrine states that all individual actual entities—from electrons to human persons—are essentially self-determining and possess a capacity for "feeling" or a degree of subjective interiority. Although all actual entities possess experience, it is not necessarily conscious experience; Whitehead argues that consciousness presupposes experience, but not vice versa. Panexperientialism is a significant departure from the dominant metaphysical theories of idealism (all is mind), dualism (mind and matter are equally fundamental), and materialism (all is matter).

The other side of the task of reconciling science and theology involves overcoming exaggerations from the religious/theology side that conflict with necessary assumptions of science, the main exaggeration of which involves the idea of divine power. Whitehead and Hartshorne do believe that a metaphysical description of reality points to the necessity of a supreme agent to which the name "God" can meaningfully be applied (arguments for the existence of God are developed more fully by Hartshorne[22] than by Whitehead). Their alternative proposal to the traditional view of divine power is that the power of God is persuasive, not coercive, with power intermediate between the omnipotent God of classical theism and the absentee God of deism.[23] With Barbour, I contend that process metaphysics is the most promising mediator between science and theology in today's academic environment.[24]

The Catholic philosopher and theologian John Haught takes pains to let science be science and to simultaneously let theology be theology. The scientific method, Haught insists, should have

21. Cf. Griffin, *Unsnarling the World-Knot*, 3–7.

22. See for example, Charles Hartshorne, *Man's Vision of God*; see also Hartshorne, *The Logic of Perfection*.

23. Cf. Whitehead, *Process and Reality*; Whitehead, *Adventures of Ideas*; and Hartshorne, *Creativity in American Philosophy*

24. Barbour, *When Science Meets Religion*, 34.

nothing to say about purpose, values, or even God's existence. Rather, it should stick to dealing with physical causes and avoid attempting to give ultimate explanations. To understand how theology may in some sense be explanatory of life's apparent designs without posing as an alternative to evolutionary accounts, one must develop what Haught calls a "layered explanation."[25] By "layered explanation," he simply means that everything in our experience can be explained at multiple levels of understanding, in distinct and noncompeting ways. The idea that there can be a plurality of compatible explanations for a single event or phenomenon is an ancient one, endorsed by great thinkers such as Socrates, Plato, Aristotle, Augustine, Aquinas, and Kant, and Haught argues that it is a valid methodology even in this age of science.

In other words, ultra-Darwinists like Dawkins and Dennett need not insist that natural selection rather than divine creativity accounts for living design. In a layered understanding, different levels of explanation are simultaneously operative. Just because natural selection can account for the apparent design of a fish's eye at one level of understanding, for example, this does not necessarily exclude divine creativity as an explanation at a deeper level. Since theology operates on a different explanatory level from—alongside of, and not in conflict with—scientific accounts of phenomena, evolutionary biologists should not expect to see divine influence intervening directly in the life-process at the level where natural selection is operative. Nor should they smugly conclude that they have ruled out divine creativity as a valid theological idea just because they see no "evidence" of direct divine manipulation in the formation of biological complexity.[26]

Moreover, thinkers from Plato to Alfred North Whitehead have acknowledged that things cannot be actualized without being patterned (or ordered) by some "formative" principle(s). In contemporary scientific usage, information is identified—at various levels—as the set of principles that organize *subordinate* elements into hierarchically distinct domains. Haught avers one dimension that gets lost

---

25. Haught, *Making Sense of Evolution*, 23.
26. Haught, *Making Sense of Evolution*, 25.

A Tripartite Contemporary Relation of Science & Theology

in modernity's simplistic reductionism is the dimension of "information," which means, he says, that more is going on in evolution than merely molecular or atomic activity. Indeed, complex organizational principles inform the more elemental levels, and he loosely assigns the term "information" to these principles, noting that information is not reducible to its constituent matter and energy.[27]

When faced with information, Haught contends, contemporary science has alighted upon something distinct from the material causes that had lent credence to reductionist views of life (and by extension, to mind). Analytically basal, the DNA molecule appears to be composed of simple "chemical components," but at a deeper level of understanding, the informational arrangement of genetic codons—A, T, C, and G—is the most significant feature of it. The specific sequence of genetic codons of entities is, after all, what determines what the entity will be phenomenologically. Chemically speaking, if one looks at DNA, he or she will not notice the informational content that the constituent atoms and molecules are carrying. However, at a deeper "reading level," the informational arrangement of the codons is all-important. My existence as a member of the Homo sapiens *sapiens* has to do not only with my evolutionary ancestry, but also with the specific sequence of nucleotides in my DNA.

Haught states that even if I descended continuously from a common ancestor, and even if my genetic makeup differs quantitatively from that of chimpanzees and bonobos by only a minute amount, the "informational" difference is great enough to produce both ontological and biological distinctiveness. In the arena of information, then, I am discontinuous with the rest of life. Even though I remain continuous with all animals at the level of my evolutionary, atomic, molecular, and metabolic constitution, the specific informational content embedded within my genes is what counts the most. It must be stressed that this informational aspect is naturally derived, with Haught stipulating that the information content is *not* an instance of "intelligent design."[28] What Haught proposes, however, is

---

27. Haught, *Making Sense of Evolution*, 50.
28. Haught, *Making Sense of Evolution*, 50–51.

A Tripartite Contemporary Relation of Science & Theology

that an awareness of the informational content "silently at work in the universe"[29] offers at least one way to understand how different levels of both being and value can descend from earlier instantiations of the evolutionary advance without being completely reducible to them (i.e., they are "emergent"—I am using the distinctively philosophical sense of the term as I have not developed in this book heretofore; however, see the footnote for references to my previously published material regarding this usage of the term).[30]

A Contemporary Relation of Science & Theology[31]

In the previous sections of chapter 1, I have attempted to explicate how one should understand the relationship between theology and science in the (late-)modern environ. In so doing, I have noted that the scientific expansionist, religious expansionist, ideological expansionist, and scientific and religious restrictionist positions all fall short of an adequate explanation of the relationship between theology and science. Additionally, I have somewhat generously updated Whitehead and Hartshorne's view of the relation between science and theology, which is demonstrable as a monistic, process-influenced view marked by an *overlapping* of the two domains. In so doing, I have highlighted the panexperientialist aspect of the process view, which implies that not just humans but even subatomic particles have a capacity for subjective interiority. Also, I noted that the other side of the process view of the relationship between science and theology involves overcoming the exaggeration of divine power, with this book opting to view God's power as one of persuasion rather than coercion.

The advocation of a monistic, process-influenced view of the overlapping relationship between science and theology is aided by

---

29. Haught, *Making Sense of Evolution*, 51.

30. McCall, "Aquinas, Teleology, and the Modern Evolutionary Synthesis," 375–95; see also McCall, "Evolution, Emergence, and Final Causality," 148–64; and McCall, "Emergence and Kenosis," 149–64.

31. For further information and details about this putative "contemporary relation of science and theology," see my own book from 2018, McCall, *Modern Relation of Theology and Science*.

A Tripartite Contemporary Relation of Science & Theology

the interaction with the sciences modeled by the history of philosophical inquiry in the Catholic tradition, which gives the method to emulate in its re-articulation of Aristotelian positions. In particular, I highlighted Haught's advocation of a layered explanation, by which he means that everything in our experience can be explained at multiple levels of understanding, in distinct and noncompeting ways. Moreover, in this chapter I examined how Haught advances the notion that information is identified in contemporary scientific usage as the set of principles that organize *subordinate* elements into hierarchically distinct domains, a concept that points to realities beyond what the principles of physics alone can explain. In sum, I view a monistic, process-influenced view of the *overlapping* relationship between science and theology as the most constructive and most tenable response to Darwinism in today's society.

I see much value, additionally, in employing science as a "handmaiden" to theology, a role first envisioned by Philo Judaeus in the first century, later expressed in medieval theology by Augustine in the fourth century, and fully embraced in the early twelfth century by Hugh of Saint-Victor. Our current Pope, Francis, in the apostolic exhortation *Evangelii Gaudium*, offers something akin to this position, writing that "The church is herself a missionary disciple; she needs to grow in her interpretation of the revealed word and in her understanding of truth. The other sciences also help to accomplish this, each in its own way."[32] I suggest that this means that the other sciences, biology for example, can critique, hone, and refine theology, thereby making it more robust. This means, then, that the Book of Nature and the Book of Revelation mutually illuminate each other, though admittedly we need to be wary of unhesitatingly attaching tenets of faith to current scientific theory, which may at any time be overturned. Pope Francis goes on to state, "For those who long for a monolithic body of doctrine guarded by all and leaving no room for nuance, this might appear as undesirable and leading to confusion. But in fact such variety serves to bring out and develop different facets of the inexhaustible riches of the gospel."[33]

---

32. Francis, *The Joy of the Gospel*, 34.
33. Francis, *The Joy of the Gospel*, 35.

A Tripartite Contemporary Relation of Science & Theology

We are also aided in our endeavor to understand science and theology in an evolutionary world by Thomas Aquinas's characterization of God working through secondary causes. Denis Edwards stipulates that Aquinas perceived God to act in and through creatures, or natural causes, enabling them to be truly causal in their own right, by enabling them to be, to act, and to become.[34] Aquinas notes that God acts through intermediaries, imparting to them the dignity of having causal powers. In respecting their dignity and integrity, God grants secondary causes their proper autonomy. Edwards points out that for Aquinas, God is "always and everywhere at work" through secondary causes.[35] I resonate with Aquinas's attempt to salvage the particularity of divine involvement in our scientifically driven world.[36] In contrast to Aquinas and the larger Catholic tradition, however, I view God to involve Godself not only primarily through secondary causality, but also *exclusively* through it,[37]

---

34. Edwards, *How God Acts*, 80–81.
35. Edwards, *How God Acts*, 81.
36. Edwards, *How God Acts*, 83; cf. Aquinas, *Summa Theologica* 1a.105.7ad1.

37. Frankly, this is one area in which I do not agree with the Catholic Church. That is, unlike it, I do not aver that there is a soul present at the moment of conception, and much less so do I agree with the Platonic idea that the soul preexists embodiment. This position of my own is based on both my personal experience in life as well as my training as a biologist. Indeed, I was involved in a head-on collision in 1995, which rendered me comatose from severe and massive brain damage. I slept as merely a Homo species for many months, kept alive by machines. After my re-emergence from the comatose state, I had to relearn everything—read, write, who I was, who my parents were, etc. There was no "ensoulment" present within my then-shallow human existence. I only "became" truly human again with a display of higher cognitive functioning in the weeks and months following my re-emergence from the coma, at the re-appearance of higher cognitive functioning. There was a "re-ensoulment," if you will. As is well known from church teaching and tradition, there was a creature into which, in the primal moments of "creation," God breathed the "breath of life," and this basal entity, I argue, is of the human form, though not fully human (perhaps these entities were Homo *heidelbergensis*, Homo *rudolfensis*, Homo *abilis*, Homo *floresiensis*, Homo *erectus*, Homo *neanderthalis*, or even Homo *sapiens idaltu*). I am able to support my contention that God works exclusively through secondary causality in part by denying the immediate derivation of the soul at conception. Though one argument against the latter position is based on the faith-view that God directly creates each human soul at the moment of conception, I dismiss

through the perhaps unknown laws of nature, much alike to Denis Edwards.[38]

---

this as a spurious position. Qualifying my position that God works exclusively through secondary causality in *material existence* would resolve the issue outright, though I do not feel persuaded by that argument. Emanationism and humanity's cooperation with grace are within the range of immediate ensoulment and the later, subsequent ensoulment of humanity. However, I tend to shy away from the theory of emanation because it—unlike our modern theory of evolution, which includes the notion that the entirety of the world is in the process of development—holds to the immutability of the *first* principle as to both *quality* and *quantity*; further, I also differ with emanationism in so much that it involves a declension of perfection of its entailments, whereas in evolution, development directly implies the movement from less to more perfect. I find the two positions, therefore, to be almost contraries to one another.

38. Edwards, *How God Acts*, 83.

PART I

Preliminary Considerations—The Secular Evolutionary Worldview (SEW)

2

The Secular Evolutionary Worldview (SEW) Defined & Explicated

A Brief Explanation of the SEW

In the following chapter, one will find an exposition of the overarching "secular evolutionary worldview" (SEW) of the biological sciences.[1] The core of the SEW is well summarized by George Gaylord Simpson:

> Man is the result of a purposeless and natural process that did not have him in mind. He was not planned. He is a state of matter, a form of life, a sort of animal, and a species of the order primates, akin nearly or remotely to all of life and indeed to all that is material.[2]

Secular science is grounded in Darwinian evolution. Carl Sagan states simply, "Evolution is a fact, not a theory."[3] Huxley claims, "The first point to make about Darwin's theory is that it is no longer a theory, but a fact . . . Darwinianism has come of age so to speak. We do no longer have to bother about establishing the fact

---

1. For further information of this SEW and its alternatives, see my own volume: McCall, *Evolution*, chapter 1, 2–33; as well as part II of said text, comprised of chapters 2, 3, and 4 (34–48, 49–63, and 64–81, respectively).
2. Simpson, *The Meaning of Evolution*, 345.
3. Sagan, *Cosmos*, 27.

of evolution."[4] Antony Flew is scandalized by the notion that there was a time, "unbelievably," when the Vatican questioned "the fact of the evolutionary origin of the species."[5]

I will first define what a worldview itself contains and connotes, for it is only after defining "worldview" appropriately that I can then shift to the individual scholars which I desire to write upon (primarily the secularists Michael Ruse[6] and Elliot Sober, though I will include five anthologies that contain works by various other authors). After defining the term "worldview," I will then highlight about a dozen topics and theses in a logical sequence, consisting of: the notion of *progress*; the entailments of *adaptation/ism*, with the sub-theses of *natural & sexual selection*, the *units of selection*, and *functions*; the process of *speciation*, with the sub-theses of *the causes of speciation* and of *species concepts*; and the idea of *common ancestry*, with the sub-thesis of *homologies*.

The meaning of the term "worldview" (also seen to be used as "world-view" or "world view" by various authors) seems self-evident: an intellectual perspective on the world or universe. But it has many characteristics. Indeed, the online edition of the Collins English Dictionary defines world-view as a "a comprehensive, esp. personal, philosophy or conception of the world and of human life."[7] The CED similarly defines the German noun *Weltanschauung*—from which we get our English term "worldview"—as "a comprehensive, esp. personal, philosophy or conception of the universe and of human life."[8] In "The Question of a *Weltanschauung*," Sigmund Freud describes it as "an intellectual construction which solves all the problems of our existence uniformly on the basis of one overriding hypothesis, which, accordingly, leaves no question

---

4. Cf. Huxley, *At Random*. See also Tax, *Evolution of Life*, 1.

5. Kurtz, *The Humanist Alternative*, 110. In an interesting development since Flew made these remarks, Dr. Flew has left his atheistic position for some form of deism.

6. Cf. my own forthcoming volume on Ruse for more information regarding his positions: McCall, *Reading Ruse*.

7. Collins English Dictionary, "Worldview."

8. Collins English Dictionary, "Weltanschauung."

The Secular Evolutionary Worldview (SEW) Defined & Explicated

unanswered and in which everything that interests us finds its fixed place."[9]

But this does not mean that the meaning of the term "worldview" as I use it here does not have other connotations, some of which I will now unpack. Indeed, notably, in the *Discipleship of the Mind*, James W. Sire defines worldview as "a set of presuppositions" which we hold "about the makeup of our world."[10] Worldview, then, represents one's most fundamental beliefs and assumptions about the universe she inhabits. It reflects how he would answer fundamental questions about who and what we are, where we came from, etc. Worldviews operate at both the individual level and the societal level.

Rarely will two people have exactly the same worldview, but within any society, certain worldview types will be represented more prominently than others, and will therefore exert greater influence on the culture of that society. The elements of one's worldview, the beliefs about certain aspects of ultimate reality, are one's:

1. *Epistemology*: which could be defined as beliefs about the nature and sources of knowledge;
2. *Metaphysics*: which could be defined as beliefs about the ultimate nature of reality;
3. *Anthropology*: which could be defined as beliefs about the nature and purpose of humanity, in general, and oneself, in particular;
4. *Axiology*: which could be defined as beliefs about the nature of value, what is good and bad, what is right and wrong;
5. *Cosmology*: which could be defined as beliefs about the origins and nature of the universe, life, and especially humanity; and one's
6. *Theology*: which could be defined as beliefs about the existence and nature of God.

It is, therefore, no mistake that secular evolutionary biology has characteristics of a classical "religion." Some evolutionists

---

9. Freud, *New Introductory Lectures in Psycho-Analysis*, 158.
10. Sire, *Discipleship of the Mind*, 136.

Part I

claim, unabashedly, that a Darwinian worldview possesses no religious content. However, this notion is not well-supported by neo-Darwinian philosophers, who themselves admit to such religious overtones within Darwinian thought. For example, Michael Ruse, a leading neo-Darwinian, states the following: "Evolution is promoted by its practitioners as more than mere science. Evolution is promulgated as an ideology, a secular religion . . . Evolution is a religion. This was true of evolution in the beginning, and it is true of evolution still today."[11]

The various definitions just given are essentially in accord with one another. However, it is in Freud's sense of the meaning of *Weltanschauung* that I use the term "worldview" in this chapter. As such, a worldview is the set of beliefs about fundamental aspects of reality that ground and influence all one's perceiving, thinking, knowing, and doing. Since the patristic era, Western civilization, largely, has been dominated by a Christian worldview. But in the last couple of centuries, for technological and theological reasons—but most explicitly the scientific ones—the traditional Christian worldview has lost its dominance, and competing worldviews have become far more prominent, including at least the following:

1. *Modernism*: all things in the physical world can be explained by "modern," scientific processes.
2. *Postmodernism*: there are very few or no objective truths and moral standards; "reality" is a human social construction.
3. *Pantheism*: God is the sum total of all reality, as each thing or entity within it is itself also divine.
4. *Pluralism*: different world religions represent equally valid perspectives on God, the ultimate reality—as such, there are many valid paths to salvation.
5. *Panentheism*: God is the totality of reality; however, while God is in all things, God is more than all things at the same time. And
6. *Ontological Naturalism*: there is no God; humans are just highly evolved animals; the universe is a closed physical system.

---

11. Ruse, "How Evolution Became a Religion."

The Secular Evolutionary Worldview (SEW) Defined & Explicated

It is this last worldview that is predominant within the biological sciences today, and which I have termed the "secular evolutionary worldview" (SEW).

Major Topics, Theses, & Sub-theses of the SEW

The Roles of & for Common Ancestry, Selection/ism, & Adaptation/ism in the SEW

First, before we move into an exposition of these terms in (macro-)evolution, with reference to the SEW, allow me to make some general statements of fact about the terms I am using herein. Allow me to start with common ancestry. It is common belief that all cellular life forms on earth have a common (i.e., shared) origin. This view is supported by the universality of the genetic code and the universal conservation of multiple genes, particularly those that encode key components of the translation system. In *On the Origin of Species*, Charles Darwin famously proposed what we may now call the universal common ancestry (UCA) hypothesis: "I should infer from analogy that probably all the organic beings which have ever lived on this earth have descended from some one primordial form, into which life was first breathed."[12] For a century after the publication of Darwin's bold proposition, before the advent of molecular biology, the UCA hypothesis remained an untested and hardly testable speculation.[13] UCA is a, if not the, central pillar of modern evolutionary theory.[14] As first suggested by Darwin,[15] the theory of common ancestry posits that all extant terrestrial organisms share a common genetic heritage, each being the genealogical

---

12. Darwin, *On the Origin of Species*, 1.
13. Cf. Koonin, "Comparative Genomics," 127–36.
14. See Sober, *Evidence & Evolution*, chapter 4.
15. See Darwin, *On the Origin of Species*, chapter 14.

Part I

descendant of a single species from the distant past.[16] The classic evidence for common ancestry includes (at least) the following:

1. Classification: This merely means that animals with similar characteristics are grouped together. For example, monkeys, apes, and humans are all in the order primates, as they have eyes in the front of the face and hands that can grasp something. These similar characteristics imply that these species are, in some sense, related.
2. Comparative anatomy: This assertion means that we must compare the structure of the body, or parts of the body, in different animals. For example, the bones of the front limbs of many mammals show "homology"—that is, there are equivalent bones that have the same basic pattern. A simple singular example of this "homology" is that most mammals and reptiles have five fingers or toes.
3. Vestigial organs/features: Vestigial organs are, simply put, organs that have no function but are inherited from a distant ancestor where they did function. For instance, the modern human appendix has no usage in us because, in part, we are no longer feeding on the same diet as our progenitors. With regard to vestigial features, for example, flightless birds still have wings, and modern humans have tail bones.
4. Embryo development: This asseveration merely highlights that mammals, birds, and reptiles proceed through a very similar stage in the embryo during which they produce a "tail" and "gill slits" (even in modern humans). This embryonic development implies that they all descended from an ancestor that had a tail and gills.
5. Biochemistry: This contention applies to the fact that all organisms contain similar molecules (proteins, fats, carbohydrates, DNA). The DNA, for instance, of closely related species is very similar: modern human and modern chimpanzee

---

16. Cf. Raup and Valentine, "Multiple Origins of Life," 2981–84; see also Crick, "The Origin of the Genetic Code," 367–79. Further, see Sober and Steel, "Testing the Hypothesis of Common Ancestry," 395–408; still further, see Dobzhansky, "Nothing in Biology Makes Sense Except in the Light of Evolution," 125–29.

The Secular Evolutionary Worldview (SEW) Defined & Explicated

DNA is about 99 percent the same. Even mammals such as mice have over 95 percent of the same genes that we do (which is why studies of new drugs start with experiments on mice and rats, by the way).
6. Biogeography: This assertion means that different parts of the world have different species. Bluntly, kangaroos and their relatives are only found in Australia because they evolved there. America has cactus plants, whereas Africa has euphorbs.
7. Fossil evidence: As we all know, fossils are the remains of organisms that have been left in soil or rock. Radiometric dating uses the radioactive decay of chemical elements to show the age of a fossil. The earliest human-like fossils are all from Africa, and date back about 6 million years. The genus Australopithecus, for example, had several species of early human-like creatures, roughly two to four million years ago. Our species, Homo sapiens *sapiens*, is much more recent, evolving roughly 150,000 years ago.
8. Selectively neutral similarities: Similarities which have no adaptive relevance cannot be explained by the concept of convergent evolution, and therefore these non-adaptive similarities provide compelling support for universal common descent.

Common ancestry is correlated with the concept of common descent, which is a term within evolutionary biology that refers to the lineal derivation of a particular group of organisms. The process of common decent involves the formation of new species from a single ancestral population. When a recent common ancestor is shared between two organisms, they are said to be closely related. In contrast, common descent can also be traced back to a universal common ancestor of all living organisms using molecular genetic methods. Such evolution from a universal common ancestor involved several speciation events as a result of natural selection and other processes, such as geographical separation.

Common descent, in fact, is a concept in evolutionary biology which is applicable when one species is the ancestor of two or more species later in time. All living beings are in fact descendants of a unique ancestor commonly referred to as the last universal common ancestor (LUCA) of all life forms on the third rock from the sun (i.e., earth), according to modern evolutionary biology.[17] Common descent is an effect of speciation in that multiple species derive from a single ancestral population. The more recent the ancestral population two species have in common, the more closely are they related. The most recent common ancestor of all currently living organisms is the last universal ancestor,[18] which lived about four billion years ago[19]

Universal common descent through an evolutionary process was proposed by the British naturalist Charles Darwin in the concluding sentence of his 1859 book *On the Origin of Species*. He writes, therein, the following:

> There is grandeur in this view of life, with its several powers, having been originally breathed into a few forms or into one; and that, whilst this planet has gone cycling on according to the fixed law of gravity, from so simple a beginning endless forms most beautiful and most wonderful have been, and are being, evolved.[20]

In the 1740s, however, the French mathematician Pierre Louis Maupertous arrived at a similar idea to the one that all organisms had a common ancestor, and had diverged through random variation and natural selection. In *Essai de cosmologie* (1750), Maupertuis noted,

> May we not say that, in the fortuitous combination of the productions of Nature, since only those creatures *could* survive in whose organizations a certain degree of adaptation was present, there is nothing extraordinary in the fact that such adaptation is actually found in all these species which now exist? Chance, one might say, turned out a vast number of individuals; a small proportion of these were organized in such a manner that the

---

17. See, for example, Weiss et al., "The Physiology and Habitat," 16,116.
18. Cf. Theobald, "A Formal Test," 219–22.
19. Cf. Steel and David, "Origins of Life," 168–69.
20. Darwin, *On the Origin of Species*, 490.

The Secular Evolutionary Worldview (SEW) Defined & Explicated

> animals' organs could satisfy their needs. A much greater number showed neither adaptation nor order; these last have all perished... Thus the species which we see today are but a small part of all those that a blind destiny has produced.[21]

Also, in 1794, Charles Darwin's own grandfather, Erasmus, asked,

> Would it be too bold to imagine, that in the great length of time, since the earth began to exist, perhaps millions of ages before the commencement of the history of mankind, would it be too bold to imagine, that all warm-blooded animals have arisen from one living filament, which the great First Cause endued with animality, with the power of acquiring new parts attended with new propensities, directed by irritations, sensations, volitions, and associations; and thus possessing the faculty of continuing to improve by its own inherent activity, and of delivering down those improvements by generation to its posterity, world without end?[22]

Charles Darwin's own views about common descent, as expressed in *On the Origin of Species*, were that it was probable that there was only one progenitor for all life forms: "Therefore I should infer from analogy that probably all the organic beings which have ever lived on this earth have descended from some one primordial form, into which life was first breathed."[23] So, then, the theory of common descent states that all living organisms are descendants of a single ancestor. Thus, the theory of common descent helps to explain why species living in different geographical regions exhibit different traits insomuch as some traits are highly conserved among broad animal classifications, and why seemingly different and disparate species share inherited physical and genetic traits. While the theory of common descent is primarily derived from the physical observation of various phenotypes (e.g., size, color, beak shape,

---

21. As cited in Harris, *Evolution*, 107.
22. Darwin, *Zoonomia*, 397.
23. Darwin, *On the Origin of Species*, 484.

Part I

embryological development, etc.), modern advances in genetics and associated molecular techniques have been able to demonstrate that the process by which DNA is eventually translated into proteins is maintained among all lifeforms. Small changes in DNA between organisms have revealed a shared ancestry as well as insight into important changes that resulted in various speciation events. Phylogenetic trees are often used to hypothesize the evolution of various organisms and shared common descent.

The "tree of life" scenario that most taxonomists currently accept is the three-domain system which Carl Woese et al. introduced in 1990.[24] According to this model, the first—most ancient and most fundamental—division of the tree of life is into three domains: archaea, bacteria, and eukarya. Archaea bacteria are ancient single-celled organisms once thought to inhabit only extreme conditions, such as salt lakes and the extreme locations of hyperthermal oceanic vents, but now are realized to be extremely common. Bacteria, in fact, are ubiquitous in nature and—for the sake of illustration—there are around ten times (10x) more bacterial cells making their home in the modern human body than there are explicitly human cells. Eukarya account for the rest of life on earth and are divided up to into five or six kingdoms, depending on which authority you follow. All animals (including humans), plants, and other organisms such as fungi and algae are eukaryotes and share a common ancestor. Further, universal common ancestry would make it true that all three domains themselves stem (or branch) from a single root.

The most splendid thing about common ancestry is that it unifies every creature, biotic or not biotic, into the same web of life, insomuch as, one could say, we "are all in this together," so to speak. From probably the most common bacteria in modern humans, Staphylococcus *aureus*, to the dog. From the bacteria to the bobo. We are all family—we all originally came from one progenitor. Succinctly, common ancestry refers to a *single species from which two or more other species are derived*.

Regarding "adaptation/ism," allow me to make some comments as well. Adaptationism, also known as functionalism, is

---

24. Woese et al., "Towards a Natural System of Organisms."

The Secular Evolutionary Worldview (SEW) Defined & Explicated

the Darwinian view that *most* physical and psychological traits of organisms are evolved adaptations. That *all* traits are adaptations is a view now shared by few biologists, however. Adaptationists perform research to try to distinguish true adaptations from byproducts or random variation. George C. Williams's 1966 book entitled *Adaptation and Natural Selection* was and is still highly influential in adaptationism's development. Adaptationism is, succinctly, an approach to studying the evolution of both form and function. Adaptationism attempts to frame both the existence and persistence of traits. Accordingly, a trait is an adaptation if it fulfils the following criteria thoroughly:

1. The trait is a variation of an earlier form.
2. The trait is heritable through the transmission of genes. And
3. The trait enhances reproductive success.

In evolutionary biology, "adaptation" refers to the process of adjusting an entity's behavior, physiology, or structure, in order to become more suited to an environment (that is, in the long run, more "fit"). Adaptation may also be defined as the state reached by the biological population undergoing adjustments or changes. It may also pertain to the *trait* that made the species a better "fit" for the environment. Thus, the trait is referred to as the "adaptive trait." Notably, the term "adaptation" comes from the Latin *"adapto,"* which means "I fit" or "I adjust to."

In evolutionary biology, the organism tends to undergo changes to become more suited or fit to its environment. For a trait to be considered as an adaptation, it has to be heritable, functional, and increases fitness. According to Charles Darwin's theory of evolution by natural selection, organisms adapt to their environment so that they can persist and pass their genes (and gene products, i.e., proteins) on to the next generation. Adaptations are essential to a species's survival. The adaptive traits that the species will acquire through time may be *structural* (i.e., physical adaptive traits), *behavioral* (e.g., vocalizations, courtship rituals, nesting, and mating), or *physiological* (e.g., developing resistance to diseases or to toxic chemicals).

"Adaptationism," as such, refers to a family of views about the importance of natural selection in the evolution of organisms, in the construction of evolutionary explanations, and in defining the goal of research on evolution. Advocates of adaptationism or "adaptationists" view natural selection among individuals within a population as the only important cause of the evolution of a trait; they also typically believe that the construction of explanations based solely on natural selection to be the most fruitful way of making progress in evolutionary biology and that this endeavor addresses the most important goal of evolutionary biology, which is to understand the evolution of adaptations. An important alternative approach, "pluralism," invokes historical contingency and developmental and genetic constraints, in addition to natural selection, as important causes of the evolution of a trait. Advocates of pluralism, or "pluralists," often also argue that the attempt to construct a natural selective explanation of a trait is not the most fruitful way to make explanatory progress and that understanding adaptation is just one of several important questions in evolutionary biology.

The "debate" over adaptationism is commonly understood to be the back-and-forth between adaptationists and pluralists. The debate over adaptationism is often traced back to a 1979 essay by Stephen Jay Gould and Richard C. Lewontin.[25] This essay is extremely important but, in fact, this debate traces back to the nineteenth century, with elements of adaptationistic pluralism as currently understood being present in the work of Henry Bates, William Bateson, Charles Darwin, Ernst Haeckel, Herbert Spencer, Alfred Russell Wallace, and August Weissman, among others.[26] Recent work in the philosophy of biology[27] has helped uncover three proverbial "flavors" of adaptationism, which reflect differences in beliefs among current evolutionary arguments. These three

---

25. Gould and Lewontin, "The Spandrels of San Marco," 581–98.

26. See, for example, Mayr, *The Growth of Biological Thought*; and Ruse, *Darwin and Design*, for more of the historical background on the concepts of adaption and adaptationism.

27. See, for example, Orzack and Sober, "Optimality Models and the Test of Adaptationism," 41–55; Amundson, "Logical Adaptationism," 505–06; Amundson, "Doctor Dennett and Doctor Pangloss," 577–84; and Godfrey-Smith, "Three Kinds of Adaptationism," 335–57.

The Secular Evolutionary Worldview (SEW) Defined & Explicated

"flavors" represent commitments about the state of nature, about the way to do science, and about what is important to study.

The first flavor of adaptationism, *empirical*, is the view that natural selection is ubiquitous, free from constraints, and provides a sufficient explanation for the evolution of most traits, which are "locally" optimal; that is, the observed trait is superior to any alternative that does not require "redefining" the organism.[28] This is a claim about realized influence of natural selection on the evolution of traits as compared to other evolutionary influences. The second flavor of adaptationism, *explanatory*, is the view that explaining traits as adaptations resulting from natural selection is the central goal of evolutionary biology. This is a claim about the greater importance of some kinds of explanations. The third flavor of adaptationism, *methodological*, is the view that looking first for adaptation via natural selection is the most efficient approach when trying to understand the evolution of any given trait. The belief that adaptations are common is quite different from the claim that only natural selection need be invoked in order to explain these adaptations.

These three "flavors" of adaptationism are logically independent. The truth of one claim does not necessarily imply the truth of the other claims. For example, it could be true that most traits are adaptations that can be explained by invoking no more than natural selection (the first flavor) but still be false that it is *most* fruitful to look first for adaptation (the third flavor). In fact, the "real" intellectual stances of those who partake in this debate are more circumscribed in that most adaptationists are advocates of empirical, explanatory, and methodological adaptationism.[29] In addition, there are many biologists who are advocates of explanatory and methodological adaptationism, but who explicitly reject empirical adaptationism.[30] On the other hand, some biologists reject all three flavors of adaptationism.[31]

---

28. Cf. Orzack and Sober, "Optimality Models and the Test of Adaptationism," 41–55.

29. See, for example, Charnov, *The Theory of Sex Allocation*; Smith, "Optimization Theory in Evolution," 31–56; and Dawkins, *The Selfish Gene*.

30. See Mayr, "How to Carry Out the Adaptationist Program?," 324–34.

31. See, for example, Carroll, *Endless Forms Most Beautiful*; Wagner et

Part I

Godfrey-Smith defines empirical adaptationism as follows: "Natural selection is a powerful and ubiquitous force, and there are few constraints on the biological variation that fuels it. To a large degree, it is possible to predict and explain the outcome of evolutionary processes by attending only to the role played by selection. No other evolutionary factor has this degree of causal importance."[32] This definition captures two important beliefs of adaptationists: first, that natural selection governs all important aspects of trait evolution and that other evolutionary influences will be of little consequence at least over the long term; second, the order in nature is a consequence of natural selection. Parker and Smith are an important example of this approach.[33]

Godfrey-Smith defines explanatory adaptationism in this way: "The apparent design of organisms, and the relations of adaptedness between organisms and their environments, are the *big questions*, the amazing facts in biology. Explaining these phenomena is the core intellectual mission of evolutionary theory. Natural selection is the key to solving these problems; selection is the *big answer*."[34] Because it answers the biggest questions, selection has unique explanatory importance among evolutionary factors. Explanatory adaptationism is viewed by its proponents as important because it organizes research to understand how natural selection underlies the world around us.[35]

Godfrey-Smith then defines "methodological" adaptationism in this way: "The best way for scientists to approach biological systems is to look for features of adaptation and good design. Adaptation is a good 'organizing concept' for evolutionary research."[36] This is a claim about the efficiency of tools, simply. No matter how

---

al., "Developmental Evolution as a Mechanistic Science," 819–31; and West-Eberhard, *Developmental Plasticity and Evolution*.

32. Godfrey-Smith, "Three Kinds of Adaptationism," 336.

33. Parker and Smith, "Optimality Theory in Evolutionary Biology," 27–33.

34. Godfrey-Smith, "Three Kinds of Adaptationism," 336.

35. See, for example, Dawkins, *The Selfish Gene*; Dennett, *Darwin's Dangerous Idea*; and Griffiths, "In What Sense does 'Nothing Make Sense Except in the Light of Evolution'?," 11–32.

36. Godfrey-Smith, "Three Kinds of Adaptationism," 337.

The Secular Evolutionary Worldview (SEW) Defined & Explicated

incorrect it may ultimately be to invoke natural selection as a sufficient explanation for a particular trait, it is the *most* direct way possible to find the true causal explanation of a trait.

In a third term that is relevant to what follows, allow me also to offer a definition of "natural selection." All populations of organisms evolve through a law-bound process, which was described by Charles Darwin in his *On the Origin of Species*. The modern explanation of this process, known as natural selection, can be briefly summarized as follows: the members of each population vary in heredity in traits of anatomy, physiology, and behavior.[37] Individuals possessing more beneficial combinations of traits survive and reproduce better than those with less beneficial combinations. As a consequence, the units that specify better physical traits—genes and chromosomes—increase in relative frequency within such populations from one generation to the next. This change in better traits, which occurs at the level of the entire population, is the essential process of both micro- and macroevolution. Although the agents of natural selection act directly on phenotypic traits and scarcely on the underlying genes (or chromosomes), the shifts they cause in the genes have lasting effects. New variation across each population arises through changes in genetic makeups, as well as their relative positions on the chromosomes.[38] Nevertheless, these changes (broadly referred to as mutations) provide only the raw material of evolution. Indeed, natural selection—differential survival and reproduction—determines the rate and direction of evolution.[39]

Although natural selection implies competition in an abstract sense between different forms of genes occupying the same chromosome positions or between different gene arrangements, pure competition, sometimes caricatured as "nature red in tooth and claw," is but one of several means by which natural selection can

---

37. Cf. Sober and Wilson, *Unto Others*, 104–05.

38. Ruse and Wilson, "Moral Philosophy as Applied Science," 555.

39. For coverage of these different components of natural selection, see the following texts: Roughgarden, *Theory of Population Genetics and Evolutionary Ecology*; Hartl and Clark, *Principles of Population Genetics*; May, *Theoretical Ecology*; and Davies and Krebs, *Behavioral Ecology*.

operate on the outer traits.[40] For followers of SEW, survival and reproduction can be promoted equally well—depending upon circumstances—through the avoidance of predators, efficient breeding, and improved cooperation with others.[41] In recent years there have been several much-publicized controversies over the pace of evolution and the universal occurrence of adaptation, which my forthcoming *Macroevolution, Contingency, & Uncontrolling, Amorepotent Love: How God Works in the (Late-)Modern World* shall explore more fully. Having offered definitions for the concepts of common ancestry, adaptation/ism and natural selection, let us now proceed forward.

Common Ancestry Revealed

SEW has a lot to state about the notion(s) of common ancestry, adaptation/ism, and selection/ism. Notably, in what follows, not only will we discuss the terms in the former sentence, but also both natural and sexual selection as main sub-theses, as well as the units of selection, with corresponding sub-theses of the *individual vs. group selection* debate, which is explicated by reference to the concept of altruism.

Why did Darwin start with an explication of natural selection, and not an exposition of what (perhaps) should be seen to be logically prior to the mechanism of diversity generation (i.e., common ancestry)? I propose that Darwin did not want to immediately offend his readers; indeed, had he started with common ancestry, his readers would have instantaneously made the mental connection between apes and humans, which he desperately wanted to avoid (at least in *On the Origin of Species*, though he later broaches that topic in his *The Descent of Man*). So, then, Darwin begins *On the Origin of Species* by noting artificial selection, then extrapolates

---

40. Ruse and Wilson, "Moral Philosophy as Applied Science," 556.

41. Salient reviews of the various modes of selection, including forms that direct individuals away from competitive behavior, can be found in Wilson, *Sociobiology*; Oster and Wilson, *Caste and Ecology in the Social Insects*; Boorman and Levitt, *The Genetics of Altruism*; and Wilson, *The Natural Selection of Populations and Communities*.

The Secular Evolutionary Worldview (SEW) Defined & Explicated

that principle to his own mechanism—natural selection—and then ends with overtures to common ancestry.

However, about 150 years after, SEW biologists can safely begin with common ancestry, for the concept of evolution in general is now more generally accepted—that is, after the "grunt work" of the mechanism of (macro-)evolution had been laid by Darwin in *On the Origin of Species*. So, then, in orienting this section, I will invert Darwin's presentation of his ideas, so as to reflect the better logical sequence, insomuch as I begin with common ancestry, and only then move to expositing both natural and sexual selection. However, it should be noted that Darwin himself says that *On the Origin of Species* is "one long argument," so perhaps it is possible that I am reading too much into his chosen arrangement of the text. But I think, truly, that I am onto something. Not only me, of course, but SEW biologists seem to think so, too. However, given how central the thesis of common ancestry is to SEW evolutionary reasoning, one might expect there to be a vast literature in which the evidence for that claim is collected and collated. But in fact, though the question is discussed, the literature upon it is hardly vast. For most SEW evolutionists, the similarities that different species share make it obvious that they have common ancestors, and there is no reason to puzzle further over the question.

Another explanation as to why Darwin put selection first in *On the Origin of Species* is provided by the thought that selection explains branching, which is given through his "Principle of Divergence."[42] It is notable that Sober prefers this alternative explanation, whereas I prefer the former.[43] In fact, Sober stipulates that there is a special feature of the relationship between common ancestry and natural selection in Darwin's theory. Natural selection and common ancestry fit well together, but only if selection has *not* been proverbially omnipotent—for if all traits evolve because there is (natural) selection for them—"Darwin's principle" would conclude that we have little or no evidence for common ancestry. Thus, what is needed is that selection causes branching *and* extinction

---

42. Darwin, *On the Origin of Species*, 26.
43. Sober, "Did Darwin Write the Origin Backwards?," 10,053.

but that some traits persist in lineages for *non*adaptive reasons. Darwin's claim that selection is not the exclusive cause of evolution plays an essential role in allowing him to develop his evidence for common ancestry.

Indeed, Darwin's conjunction of common ancestry and natural selection would be unknowable, according to "Darwin's principle," if the second conjunct described the only cause of phenotypic evolution. In broad outline, Sober notes, the evidential structure of Darwin's argument for his theory of common ancestry plus natural selection proceeds in this manner: 1) The argument for common ancestry, where neutral and deleterious phenotypes (i.e., vestigial organs, embryology, biogeography) do the main work; 2) It follows from (1) that populations have evolved across species boundaries; and 3) The argument that natural selection is an important part of the explanation of many adaptive traits, and artificial selection and the Malthusian argument for the power of selection are important, as are Darwin's many examples of adaptive phenotypes in nature. The order in *On the Origin of Species* has (3) first, and then (1), with (2) more or less implied.[44]

That being said, Darwin tells us in *On the Origin of Species* that when it comes to finding evidence for common ancestry, the adaptive features that provide evidence for natural selection are precisely where one ought *not* to look:

> Adaptive characters, although of the utmost importance to the welfare of the being, are almost valueless to the systematist. For animals belonging to two most distinct lines of descent may readily become adapted to similar conditions and thus assume a close external resemblance; but such resemblances will not reveal—will rather tend to conceal their blood-relationship to their proper lines of descent.[45]

That humans and gorillas have tailbones, and that human fetuses and fish have gill slits, are both evidence for common ancestry precisely because tailbones and gill slits are useless in modern-day

---

44. Sober, "Did Darwin Write the Origin Backwards?," 10,054.
45. Darwin, *On the Origin of Species*, 427.

humans. In contrast, the torpedo shape that sharks and dolphins share is (still) useful to both groups; understanding the concept of natural selection, one might expect this trait to evolve in large aquatic predators whether or not they have a common ancestor. This is why the adaptive similarity is insignificant to the systematist. Elliot Sober calls this "Darwin's principle," which asserts that "adaptive similarities provide almost no evidence for common ancestry while similarities that are useless or deleterious provide strong evidence for common ancestry."[46] This principle, I aver, is important to grasp and apply in our talk of common descent, adaptions, and the concept of evolutionary convergence, a topic that my forthcoming *Macroevolution, Contingency, & Uncontrolling, Amorepotent Love: How God Works in the (Late-)Modern World* shall expound upon.

The Darwinian reconstruction of the history of phenotypic evolution uses the fact of common ancestry to infer the states of lineal ancestors from the states of collateral descendants. Parsimony considerations, applied to an independently attested phylogeny, of course also play an important role in testing hypotheses about natural selection. Take the example of the hypothesis that land vertebrates evolved four limbs to help them walk on dry land: biologists reject this hypothesis because the morphological phenotype was present in the lineage *before* vertebrates emerged out of the water. Why is such a contention palatable? I suspect it is because the phenotypes of collateral descendants allow one to infer the traits of lineal ancestors. So, then, we infer from modern-day organisms (and from fossils) that the ancestors of land vertebrates had four limbs before vertebrates emerged upon dry land; thus, tetrapody evolved before walking in the vertebrate line—that is, in the sea. Darwin himself hints at this idea in *On the Origin of Species*, speaking of skull sutures:

> The sutures in the skulls of young mammals have been advanced as a beautiful adaptation for aiding parturition, and no doubt they facilitate, or may be indispensable for this act; but as sutures occur in the skulls of young birds and reptiles, which have only to escape from a broken

---

46. Sober, "Did Darwin Write the Origin Backwards?," 10,051.

egg, we may infer that this structure has arisen from the laws of growth, and has been taken advantage of in the parturition of the higher animals.[47]

Moreover, if we think of an ancestor as a species, we need to say what a species is; that is, we need to solve the notorious "species problem." One warning sign that this is not a path down which we should choose to tread is that the much-admired biological species concept[48] says that a species is a group of organisms that interbreed among themselves but which are reproductively isolated from other such groups. Understood in this way, a species must be made of sexual organisms. However, evolutionists agree that sexuality is a derived character: first there were asexual organisms. This means that the biological species concept is not the right choice if we wish to say that all life on Earth derives from a single species.[49] But the common ancestry hypothesis says that all current life forms derive from a single organism, not a single species. An organism must be alive, of course. Darwin and present-day Darwinians would not be satisfied if all life on Earth derived from the same large slab of rock whose nonliving materials produced numerous separate start-ups of life that never melded together but instead led separately to the several groups of organisms we now observe.[50] After all, your grandparents produced your parents, and your parents produced this generation; ergo your grandparents are among your ancestors.

But what is this begetting relation? It is natural to think of reproduction in terms of genetic transmission. You, for example, received half your nuclear genes from your mother and half from your father, and they, in turn, received half of their genes from each of their parents. However, it does *not* follow that you received one-quarter of your genes from each of your four grandparents. Instead, meiosis is a proverbial lottery, as one (or more) of your grandparents may have lost, meaning that you received exactly zero genes from him or her. As we consider ancestors of ours who are

47. Darwin, *On the Origin of Species*, 197.
48. Mayr, "Biology in the Twenty-First Century," 895–97.
49. Cf. Sober, *Evidence & Evolution*, 268.
50. Sober, *Evidence & Evolution*, 269.

The Secular Evolutionary Worldview (SEW) Defined & Explicated

more and more remote, it becomes increasingly certain that some of them passed no genes at all to us. Ancestors have a shot at contributing genes to their descendants, but there is no guarantee that they succeed in doing so.[51]

Selection itself causes branching and extinction, which means that selection does explain why the life around us traces back to "four or five original progenitors."[52] SEW historians who study Darwin's work often say that he thought that natural selection is analogous to an agent (see, for example, Ospovat[53] and Young[54]). Of course, it isn't literally true that natural selection is "trying" to do anything or that it "chooses" who shall live and who shall die. Selection, after all, is a mindless process. But Darwin found the idea of natural selection as an agent useful, and so have evolutionary biologists up to the present, in thinking about what natural selection would achieve by thinking about what agents would achieve if they had certain aims and if their choices were limited to a given set of feasible options.[55] In view of such, the reason antelopes don't have machine guns with which to repel the attacks of lions is not that guns would not be useful; rather, this option was not available to them ancestrally.[56] Selection selects only among those options that are actually represented in a population. It is important to remember that what is conceivable to an intelligent agent can differ from what is biologically possible for a species given its history.[57]

Another explanation may be phylogenetic inertia. Regarding phylogenetic inertia, consider the following remark by Roger Lewin:

---

51. Cf. Sober, *Evidence & Evolution*, 269.
52. Darwin, *On the Origin of Species*, 484.
53. Cf. Ospovat, *The Development of Darwin's Theory*.
54. Cf. Young, *Darwin's Metaphor*.
55. On discussion of how this "heuristic of personification" can lead one astray, however, see Sober, "Three Differences Between Evolution and Deliberation," 408–22.
56. Cf. Davies and Krebs, *Behavioral Ecology*.
57. Cf. Sober, *Evidence & Evolution*, 191.

Part I

> Why do most land vertebrates have four legs? The seemingly obvious answer is that this arrangement is the optimal design. This response would ignore, however, the fact that the fish that were ancestral to terrestrial animals also have four limbs, or fins. Four limbs may be very suitable for locomotion on dry land, but the real reason that terrestrial animals have this arrangement is because their evolutionary predecessors possessed the same pattern.[58]

There are two points that this passage suggests: the first is a simple chronological point—since the aquatic ancestors of land vertebrates already had four limbs, it is false that the trait initially became common in the lineage because of its utility for walking on dry land.[59] While this is no more controversial than the thought that cause must precede effect, once this point is granted, there is a second and more contentious thesis to reckon with, which is the claim that the correct explanation for why land vertebrates are tetrapods consists in the fact that their ancestors had four limbs—summarily, it is incorrect to maintain that the trait remained in place because there was selection for the trait due to the fact that it facilitated walking on dry land. Selection for the ability to walk on dry land of course does not explain the initial evolution of the tetrapod morphology; the question is whether, rather, the thesis that selection for walking was responsible for the trait's subsequent maintenance also should be rejected. The term "phylogenetic inertia" is sometimes used to refer to the explanation that Lewin favors, which might better be called "ancestral influence."[60]

The word "inertia," seemingly, could misleadingly suggest that lineages have a tendency to continue evolving in a certain direction even after the initial "push" that got them started is no longer present. For example, if selection initially favors the evolution of longer fur in polar bears and evolution is "inertial," then fur length will continue to increase even if there ceases to be selection for longer

---

58. Lewin, "Evolutionary Theory Under Fire," 886.

59. Cf. Eaton, "The Aquatic Origin of Tetrapods," 115–20; and Edwards, "Two Perspectives on the Evolution of the Tetrapod Limb," 235–54.

60. Cf. Sober, *Evidence & Evolution*, 244. See also Wilson, *Sociobiology*; see further Harvey and Pagel, *The Comparative Method in Evolutionary Biology*.

The Secular Evolutionary Worldview (SEW) Defined & Explicated

fur. At the start of the twentieth century, the orthogenetic theory of evolution held that inertia in this sense explains why the Irish elk had such enormous horns; this view of evolution, however, is dubious, and inertia in this sense is not what "phylogenetic inertia" is now taken to mean.

The hypothesis of phylogenetic inertia and the hypothesis of stabilizing selection propose to explain the character state of a descendant in different ways; the former appeals to the lineage's ancestral state while the latter cites processes that the lineage has subsequently in the future. Why are these two possible explanations in conflict? Cannot phylogenetic inertia and stabilizing selection both help explain why land vertebrates now have four limbs? This is not the position that Lewin takes in the quoted passage: phylogenetic inertia is said to be "the real reason"; not only is selection not the *whole* story; it isn't even *part* of the story. Lewin seems to posit that the hypothesis of phylogenetic inertia should be regarded as innocent until proven guilty, whereas the default assumption should be that ancestral influence is the right explanation unless the data force us to abandon that hypothesis.[61]

If what we observe is consistent with the hypothesis of phylogenetic inertia and also with the hypothesis of stabilizing selection, we should prefer the former, and even more, if considerations of parsimony also suggest that we should prefer the one-factor inertia explanation over a pluralistic explanation that cites both inertia and selection.[62] Other evolutionary biologists have espoused other principles of default reasoning. Whereas George C. Williams asserts that adaptation is an onerous concept that should be embraced only if the data force one to do so, Ernst Mayr takes the opposite stance— that is, only after all possible selection explanations of a given trait have been explored and rejected can one tentatively conclude that the trait is a product of drift.[63] Default principles also have been defended that give precedence to some types of natural selection over others. Williams maintains that the hypothesis of group selection

61. Notably, Ridley, *The Explanation of Organic Diversity*, recommends this policy.

62. Sober, *Evidence & Evolution*, 245.

63. Mayr, *Towards a New Philosophy of Biology*, 150–51.

is more onerous (by which he means less parsimonious) than the hypothesis of individual selection; our default assumption should be that when a trait evolves by natural selection, it evolves because it is advantageous to the individuals who possess it, not because it helps the groups in which it occurs.

Adaptationism Asserted

Adaptationism, as a claim about nature, is a thesis about the "power" of natural selection.[64] Those who debate its truth do not doubt the tree of life hypothesis; rather, the dispute concerns the mechanism, *not* the fact, of evolution. Adaptationists are inclined to answer this question in the negative; their approach to the evolution of a trait avers that natural selection is so powerful regarding a population's evolution that such complications may safely be ignored. Indeed, adaptationists tend to expect nature to conform to the predictions of well-motivated models in which natural selection is the only factor described. They expect, for example, antelopes to be *fast* rather than *slow* (if *fast* is, indeed, the fitter phenotype).

Adaptationists well realize that which phenotype is fittest depends on the biological details. Another qualification is needed in conjunction with the word "fittest": adaptationists might expect antelopes to evolve from *slow* to *fast* but will not expect them to evolve machine guns with which to counter lion attacks. When adaptationists say that the fittest trait will evolve and survive, they mean the fittest traits *already present in the population*, not the fittest of all the traits we can imagine. Although adaptationists recognize that the outcome of selection is limited by the variation available, they expect that range to be quite rich. Natural selection will optimize with respect to *existing* variation, and it is reasonable to expect the existing variation to be rich. Still, no adaptationist holds that variation is *limitlessly* rich.

Adaptationism is a "tendency" of thought for followers of SEW. In practice, its proponents often hold that variation is less constraining than critics of adaptationism are inclined to maintain.

---

64. Sober, *Philosophy of Biology*, 120.

The Secular Evolutionary Worldview (SEW) Defined & Explicated

An extreme adaptationist, for example, will conject that *every* trait evolves independently of every other, whereas an extreme anti-adaptationist will hold that *every* trait is enmeshed in a web of correlations that makes it impossible to change a part without systematically changing the whole. Practicing biologists rarely occupy either extreme, according to Sober.[65] Sober distinguishes three theses about the relevance that natural selection has to explaining why the individuals in some population X possess some trait T:

- 1. (U) Natural selection played some role in the evolution of T in the lineage leading to X.

- 2. (I) Natural selection was an important cause of the evolution of T in the lineage leading to X.

- 3. (O) Natural selection was the only important cause of the evolution of T in the lineage leading to X.[66]

These theses are presented in ascending order of logical strength; (I) entails (U) but not conversely, and (O) entails (I) but not conversely. If (I) is true, then an explanation of the trait's evolution *cannot* omit natural selection; if (O) is true, then an explanation of the trait *can* safely ignore the nonselective factors that were in play. Adaptationism, as Sober understands the term, is committed to something like (O).[67] For adaptationists, models that focus on selection and ignore the role of nonselective factors provide *sufficient explanations*. Having described what it is to endorse adaptationism with respect to a single trait in a single lineage, Sober then addresses the question of what adaptationism means *in general*. Adaptationists usually restrict their thesis to phenotypic characters; they often are prepared to concede that (O) and even (I) may be false with respect to molecular characters,[68] which makes it reasonable to formulate adaptationism as follows:

---

65. Sober, *Philosophy of Biology*, 121.

66. This paragraph's statements are originally from Orzack and Sober, "Optimality Models," 361–80, as cited in Sober, *Philosophy of Biology*, 123.

67. Sober, *Philosophy of Biology*, 123.

68. Cf. Smith, "Optimization Theory in Evolution," 31–56.

Part I

Adaptationism: Most phenotypic traits, at least in *most* populations, can be effectively explained by a model in which selection is explicated and nonselective processes are effectually ignored.[69]

Notably, the above quasi-definition of adaptationism is a generalization of (O); similar generalizations of (U) and (I) also are possible (e.g., the more general form of (U) says that natural selection is *ubiquitous*). Adaptationism, as Sober construes it, does not demand that the process of natural selection maximize the fitness of most of the organisms (or the genes) in a population.[70] As is demonstrable in the problem of altruism, natural selection can also reduce fitness. Adaptationism emphasizes the importance of natural selection; it is not committed to the thesis that natural selection always improves the level of adaptedness. Stronger versions of the adaptationism enunciated above can be obtained by replacing one or both occurrences of "most" with "all" in the above quasi-definition given of it. The result of these substitutions would be to make adaptationism more falsifiable. If adaptationism were the claim that natural selection suffices to explain *all* phenotypic traits in *all* populations, a single counterexample would be enough to refute it. However, few biologists would be prepared to endorse this strong form of the thesis. The formulation that Sober suggests, though more difficult to test, is closer to the real issue that currently distresses biologists.[71]

It is commonly asserted, in genetics circles, that phenotypic variation must reflect genetic variation. SEW adaptationists by and large are inclined to maintain that if a phenotype were to become advantageous, then some gene combination coding for that alternative trait would probably—somehow!—arise (via mutation or recombination); although this assumption is not always correct, it is more true than not. Indeed, adaptationists expect traits that have a significant influence on an organism's viability and fertility to be optimal. If *fast antelopes* are fitter than *slow antelopes*, then present-day antelopes should be *fast*. This expectation may be mistaken if

---

69. This is adapted from Sober, *Philosophy of Biology*, 124. I admit my dependence upon him freely.

70. Sober, *Philosophy of Biology*, 124.

71. Sober, *Philosophy of Biology*, 124.

the population has recently experienced a major change in its environment; indeed, if this has occurred, then the population may not have had sufficient time for the optimal phenotype to evolve (in this case, the traits one presently observes are *sub*optimal). Natural selection may be powerful, but even the most committed adaptationist will admit that it can lag behind extremely rapid ecological change;[72] after all, it takes time for novel variant traits to arise and more time still for those traits to be fixed in the population.

However, adaptationism has been criticized for being "too easy."[73] Suppose an adaptationist explanation is invented for trait T in population X and that we then find evidence against this explanation. The committed adaptationist can modify the discredited model or replace it with a different adaptationist account. Indeed, adaptationism seems to be so flexible a doctrine that it can be maintained no matter how many specific models are invented and refuted. The criticism lodged here is that adaptationism is, itself, *unfalsifiable*: The complaint is not that adaptationism is a false scientific doctrine but that it is not a scientific claim at all—that is, not meeting the Popperian definition of science. But, according to Sober, *existence* claims cannot be falsified, in the Popperian sense, by their very definition.[74]

Curiously, it is not just the critics of adaptationism who have asserted that empirical investigations do not test the hypothesis of adaptationism. Indeed, even some advocates of it have stipulated such. For example, Parker and Smith say that when the optimality approach is used to address questions like, "Why do dung flies copulate for thirty-six minutes? . . . the question is assumed to have an adaptive answer."[75] Likewise, Krebs and Davies make it quite clear that one of their "main *assumptions* is that animals are well adapted to their environments . . . We are not testing whether animals are adapted," but "rather the question we shall ask . . . is how does a

---

72. Cf. Smith, *Evolution and the Theory of Games*.

73. Sober, *Philosophy of Biology*, 130.

74. Sober, *Philosophy of Biology*, 130.

75. Parker and Smith, "Optimality Theory in Evolutionary Biology," 27–33, italics added.

particular behavior contribute to the animal's inclusive fitness?"[76] According to critics and defenders alike, then, adaptationism seems to be an assumption rather than a hypothesis *per se*.

But . . . what should we make of the claim that adaptationism is *unfalsifiable*? Sober remarks that we must, first, be careful to distinguish *propositions* from *persons*.[77] Assuredly, some adaptation*ists* have been dogmatic; perhaps some have even been unwilling to consider the possibility that there might be nonadaptive explanations; but this says nothing about the falsifiability of the propositions they hold. Whether adaptation*ism* is falsifiable is a quite separate question from how adaptation*ists* behave. The next thing Sober notes about the thesis of adaptationism is that it does not have a series of singular "crucial experiments."[78] As such, there is no single observation that could refute the thesis, even if it is false. The word "most" that appears in the thesis above is enough to ensure that there can be no "crucial experiment" at all. In addition, the quasi-thesis stipulated above says that for most traits in most species, there exists a selective explanation. As noted above, existence claims are not falsifiable in Popper's sense.

The fact that adaptationism is not falsifiable in the Popperian sense does not mean that it is not a scientific statement; instead, it means that there is more to science than is countenanced by Popperian philosophy. Adaptationism is like other *-isms* in science: for example, behaviorism in psychology and functionalism in cultural anthropology. Adaptationism is testable only in the *long run*.[79] Its plausibility—or lack thereof—cannot be decided in advance of detailed investigations of different *traits* in different *populations*. Contrariwise, biologists investigating a specific trait in a particular population are engaged in a process in which models are developed and tested against an ever-expanding body of data. It is not impermissible that in the *long run*, biologists will arrive at biologically well-motivated explanations of various traits. If biologists

---

76. Davies and Krebs, *Behavioural Ecology*, 26–27, italics added.

77. Sober, *Philosophy of Biology*, 130.

78. Sober, *Philosophy of Biology*, 130.

79. This little allusion to the phrase "*long run*," which is frequently used by C. S. Peirce, is intentional.

can do this, we then will be able to survey the body of results and decide how often adaptationist explanations turned out to be true; however, as Sober notes, the idea that we must decide is whether adaptationism is true *before* we begin the project of constructing and testing specific adaptationist explanations, which puts the cart before the horse.[80]

Although no singular observation will determine whether adaptationism is true, this does not mean that the thesis has no scientific importance. Generalizations about how evolution proceeds are of considerable scientific interest. Adaptationism is, so to speak, a "monistic" approach to the evolutionary process; the alternative to it is "pluralism," which holds that evolution is caused by a number of mechanisms of roughly coequal importance.[81] If adaptationism were unfalsifiable by scientific inquiry, however, pluralism would be unfalsifiable as well. Sober strongly contends that adaptationism is first and foremost a *research program*; after all, its core claims receive support if specific adaptationist hypotheses turn out to be well confirmed.[82] Only time will tell whether adaptationism deserves the fate of phrenology, for example.[83]

Natural Selection Explicated

According to Ruse and Wilson, both in the SEW camp, these uncertainties should not obscure the key facts about organic evolution: that it occurs as a universal process among all kinds of organisms; that the dominant driving force is natural selection; and that the observed major patterns of change are consistent with the known

---

80. Sober, *Philosophy of Biology*, 130.

81. For this point, cf. Gould and Lewontin, "The Spandrels of San Marco," 581–98, who perhaps successfully decried the hegemony of adaptationism in biology. But for a hearty defense of adaptationism, see Cain, "The Perfection of Animals," 3–29, who endorses a strong form of the adaptationist thesis. The anthologies edited by Rose and Lauder, *Adaptation*; and by Orzack and Sober, *Adaptation and Optimality*, collect a number of papers on the testing of adaptationist models.

82. Cf. Sober, *Philosophy of Biology*, 131.

83. Cf. Mitchell and Valone, "The Optimization Research Program," 43–52.

principles of molecular biology and genetics.[84] According to them, such is the view held by the vast majority of the biologists who work on heredity and evolution. Ruse and Wilson simply state that there are no such crises. They cite Motoo Kimura, the principal architect of the "neutralist" theory of genetic diversity—which proposes that most evolution at the molecular level happens through random factors—because *even he* allows that classical evolution theory has demonstrated that the basic mechanism for adaptive evolution is natural selection acting on variations produced by changes in chromosomes and genes. Such considerations as population size and structure, availability of ecological opportunities, change of environment, life cycle strategies, interaction with other species, and—to some degree—kin and group selection play a large role in our understanding of the process.[85]

Natural & Sexual Selection in Speciation

Although it was always his *major* mechanism, natural selection was *never* Darwin's *sole* mechanism of evolutionary change.[86] Further, Darwin was always a Lamarckian, in the sense of believing in the inheritance of acquired characteristics. Darwin's most prominent secondary mechanism was sexual selection: even in the earliest drafts of his theory, Darwin mentioned this kind of selection;[87] thereafter, within the *Origin*, he spelt it out, albeit without developing it; and then in his seminal work on humanoids, *The Descent of Man*, Darwin broached sexual selection in great detail, both as it applies through the animal world and as it applies to Homo sapiens *sapiens*. Ruse argues that not only was artificial selection crucial in Darwin's getting to this kind of selection, but it was essential for the place that Darwin gave it in his theorizing; in other words, without

---

84. Ruse and Wilson, "Moral Philosophy as Applied Science," 556.
85. Cf. Kimura, *The Neutral Theory of Molecular Evolution*.
86. Ruse, *Evolutionary Naturalism*, 25.
87. Cf. Darwin and Wallace, "On the Tendency of Species to Form Varieties," 46–62.

understanding Darwin's route to discovery via artificial selection, one cannot understand the structure of Darwin's argument.[88]

Moreover, Michael Ruse claims that while sexual selection is not itself subjective, Darwin's treating it as an independent kind of selection is. First, there is the historical question of how Darwin got to sexual selection. There are hints of sexual selection in the evolutionary meanderings of Darwin's grandfather, Erasmus Darwin, as well as in the writings of others that Darwin read.[89] However, study of what Darwin produced makes it certain that the key to discovery for Darwin rested in the analogy from the domestic world and the individual breeder's power of selection.[90] Breeders, after all, select for two things: 1) attributes of animals and plants that are useful to us humans; and 2) attributes that are pleasurable to us humans. It was this division that gave rise to the natural and sexual selection dichotomy.[91] In nature, these translated for Darwin into sexual selection through male combat and sexual selection through female choice.[92] One can see therefore that the analogy from artificial selection played a powerful role for Darwin when he came to introduce and justify sexual selection in the *Origin* and in later works.

Units of Selection Explained

In biology, the debate over units of selection has centered on the evolution of seemingly altruistic behaviors that benefit others at the expense of the self; this is the paradox that makes altruism such an enthralling subject for biologists. As humans, we would like to think that altruism can evolve, whereas as biologists we see animal behaviors that appear altruistic in nature, yet almost by definition it appears that natural selection will act against them.[93] What has hap-

88. Ruse, *Evolutionary Naturalism*, 25.

89. See, for example, Sebright, *The Art of Improving Breeds*; and Darwin, *The Temple of Nature*.

90. Cf. Ghiselin, *The Triumph of the Darwinian Method*.

91. Ruse, *Evolutionary Naturalism*, 26.

92. Ruse, *Evolutionary Naturalism*, 29.

93. Cf. Wilson, "Levels of Selection," 65.

Part I

pened to produce this interesting—and counterintuitive—result? First, there must be more than one group; in fact, there must be a population of groups. The groups cannot all have the same proportion of altruistic types, second, for then the results would not differ from a singular group; indeed, the groups must vary in the proportion of altruistic types.

Third, there must be a direct relationship between the proportion of altruists and the total amount of offspring produced by the group: altruistic groups need to be fitter than groups without altruists. Indeed, in order to be sufficient, the differential fitness of altruist groups must be great enough to counter the differential fitness of individuals within groups, that is, that which "naturally" selects and/or favors the selfish types.[94] Cheap individualism is meaningless, however, and no one explicitly endorses it. Even the most ardent individualists, such as George C. Williams,[95] Richard Dawkins,[96] and John Maynard Smith,[97] believe that there is something outside individual selection called group selection that in principle can evolve altruistic traits. Nevertheless, the history of individual selection from 1960 to the present day has been a "slow slide" from valid individualism to cheap individualism.[98]

However, what is good for the individual can—and does!—conflict with what is good for the group; one's adaptation concept should reflect this fact. Rather than use "individual adaptation" as an all-encompassing label that is defined so that it applies to all adaptations regardless of whether they evolve by group or individual selection, Sober thinks it to be more useful to use "group adaptation" to name traits that evolve when group selection dominates the selection process and "individual adaptation" to name traits that evolve when individual selection dominates the selection process.[99] After all, why have two labels if one of them applies no matter what?

94. Cf. Wilson, "Levels of Selection," 65.
95. Williams, "A Defense of Reductionism in Evolutionary Biology," 1–27.
96. See, for example, Dawkins, *The Selfish Gene*; and Dawkins, *The Extended Phenotype*.
97. Smith, "How to Model Evolution," 117–31.
98. Wilson, "Levels of Selection," 66.
99. Sober, *Did Darwin Write the Origin Backwards?*, 176.

The Secular Evolutionary Worldview (SEW) Defined & Explicated

One of the main questions that has exercised philosophers writing about the units of selection problem in the twentieth century is *realism* versus *conventionalism*.[100] The realist view of the evolution of a trait notes that it is a factual question whether the evolution of a trait is influenced by selection at each of several levels—group and individual. Conventionalists—like Cassidy;[101] Sterelny and Kitcher;[102] Kitcher, Sterelny, and Waters;[103] Sterelny and Griffiths;[104] and Waters[105]—argue that the biological facts alone do not settle the matter. For them, the question concerns which type of explanation has the most utility. Conventionalists acknowledge that it is sometimes true that a trait evolves because of group or individual selection. But, for conventionalists, there is a pragmatic point in favor of a *genic* selection account (not herein expanded upon by me, note)—its generality. Conventionalism is *not* the position promoted by early foes of group selection such as Williams;[106] Smith;[107] and Dawkins;[108] who argued that group selection hypotheses are factually false claims about nature.[109]

Sober describes the alternative to realism as *conventionalism*, not pluralism, because realism about units of selection and pluralism about explanation are compatible. Or, at least, he hopes they are, because he embraces them both; indeed, the explanatory pluralism that he endorses holds that, for any event, there are different true stories that explain why the event occurred.[110] Some describe more proximate causes while others describe causes that are more

100. Sober, *Did Darwin Write the Origin Backwards?*, 164.
101. Cassidy, "Philosophical Aspects of the Group Selection Controversy," 575–94.
102. Sterelny and Kitcher, "The Return of the Gene," 339–60.
103. Kitcher et al., "The Illusory Riches of Sober's Monism," 158–61.
104. Cf. Sterelny and Griffiths, *Sex and Death*.
105. Cf. Waters, "Why Genic and Multilevel Selection Theories Are Here to Stay"; cf. Waters, "Tempered Realism about Units of Selection," 553–73.
106. Cf. Williams, *Adaptation and Natural Selection*.
107. Smith, "Group Selection and Kin Selection," 1145–46.
108. Cf. Dawkins, *The Selfish Gene*.
109. Sober, *Did Darwin Write the Origin Backwards?*, 164.
110. Sober, *Did Darwin Write the Origin Backwards?*, 165.

Part I

distal; some describe macro-causes while others describe causes that are more "micro" in their orientation.[111] Notably, Philip Kitcher claims that "one can tell all the facts about how genotype and phenotype frequencies change across the generations—including the causal explanations of the changes—without any commitment to a definite level at which selection acts."[112] Notice that Kitcher does not reject the factuality of causal talk in general; he is specific in that he thinks that causal explanations can be given without invoking a uniquely correct "level."[113]

Unlike the conventionalist philosophers just discussed, the biologists West, Griffin, and Gardner;[114] Gardner and Grafen;[115] and Wild, Gardner, and West[116] do not deny that it is a factual question whether groups are ever units of selection. They agree with the viewpoint described by Sober, that group selection means fitness variation among groups and individual selection means fitness variation within groups, and that it is a factual question what the pattern of fitness variation is in a given case.[117] However, these authors argue that units of selection must be distinguished from units of adaptation and that multilevel selection theorists fail to recognize this distinction, which leads them to fall into a "logical error."[118] These authors point out that multilevel selection models of the evolution of selfishness and altruism that separately represent the contributions of individual and group selection are predictively equivalent with models of kin selection that describe the inclusive

---

111. Cf. Jackson and Pettit, "In Defense of Explanatory Ecumenism," 1–22; cf. Sober, *The Nature of Selection*; and Sober, "The Multiple Realizability Argument," 542–64.

112. Gasper, "An Interview with Philip Kitcher," 89.

113. Sober, *Did Darwin Write the Origin Backwards?*, 168.

114. West, Griffin, and Gardner "Social Semantics," 415–32.

115. Gardner and Grafen, "Capturing the Superorganism," 659–71.

116. Wild et al., "Adaptation and the Evolution of Parasite Virulence," 983–86.

117. Sober, *Did Darwin Write the Origin Backwards?*, 169.

118. Gardner and Grafen, "Capturing the Superorganism," 660.

fitnesses of the two traits; these kin selection models do not separate individual from group selection.[119]

Individual vs. Group Selection Differentiated

The units of selection problem, since it concerns the kinds of adaptations found in nature, concerns the kinds of selection processes that produced the traits that are observed.[120] Almost all of Darwin's selectionist explanations employ the concept of individual, not group, selection. A trait that evolved because it benefited the organisms that possessed it is an *individualist* adaptation; if it evolved because it benefited the groups in which it was found, then it is a *group* adaptation. Two features of these definitions are worth noting: first, the units of selection issue concerns evolutionary history, *not* current utility or usage. Groups may now possess various traits that help them avoid extinction, but it is a separate issue whether those traits evolved *because* they had that effect. If they evolved for another reason, then those traits provide an incidental *group* benefit and are not *group* adaptations. The second point is that the definition allows that different traits may have evolved for different reasons and that a single trait may have evolved for several reasons. Perhaps one trait is an individualistic adaptation, while another is a group adaptation, and that even in the same organism. In addition, it is possible for a given trait to evolve because it simultaneously benefits objects at several levels of organization.[121]

There is an interesting passage in the *Origin* where Darwin provides a general description of the traits that selection will cause to evolve. He says the following in the first edition (1859):

> In social animals it [natural selection] will adapt the structure of each individual for the benefit of the community; if each in consequence profits by the selected change.[122]

---

119. Gardner and Grafen, "Capturing the Superorganism," 660.
120. Sober, *Philosophy of Biology*, 89.
121. Sober, *Philosophy of Biology*, 90.
122. Darwin, *On The Origin of Species*, 87.

Part I

But what does the second occurrence of "each" refer to in the above passage? For Sober, evidently, it refers back to each individual.[123] If so, Darwin is merely saying that traits will evolve in benefit the group if they also—by chance—benefit the individuals who possess those traits; however, the passage does not say that traits that benefit the group will evolve because they benefit the group—as such, there is no explicit endorsement of group selection in this sentence. Notably, Darwin kept this sentence as it was for the first four editions of *On the Origin of Species*, but he apparently grew to think that it needed to be rephrased. While working on *The Descent of Man*, he prepared the changes that would appear in the fifth edition of *On the Origin of Species*, published in 1869. His adjustment to the sentence above is modest but significant:

> In social animals it [natural selection] will adapt the structure of each individual for the benefit of the whole community; if this in consequence profits by the selected change.[124]

After *The Descent of Man* appeared in 1871, Darwin toys with the sentence again. Indeed, in the sixth edition of *On the Origin of Species* (1872), he changes it to read:

> In social animals it [natural selection] will adapt the structure of each individual for the benefit of the community; if the community profits by the selected change.[125]

At this time (1872), seemingly, Darwin is openly endorsing the role of group selection, insomuch as traits that benefit the group are favored by natural selection because they benefit the group.[126] To explain the traits of individuals that promote sociality, Darwin was eager to endorse group selection, at least post-*The Descent of Man* (1871 onwards). However, there are many traits in nature that are not like sociality. So, then, Darwin's mature theory of natural

---

123. Sober, *Did Darwin Write the Origin Backwards?*, 82.
124. Darwin, *On the Origin of Species*, 172.
125. Darwin, *On the Origin of Species*, 172.
126. Cf. Richards, *Darwin and the Emergence of Evolutionary Theories*, 217.

selection begins with the idea of individual selection, but it does not end where it begins.

Altruism: Instances of Group Selection Exemplified

While the concept of altruistic behavior in everyday language seemingly necessitates an element of both motive and action, evolutionary biologists define altruism solely in terms of differential survival and reproduction.[127] The question of whether and how altruism can evolve has received an enormous amount of attention from evolutionary biologists. Edward O. Wilson even called it "the central theoretical problem of sociobiology."[128] In fact, Wilson popularized the term "sociobiology" (which I will not pontificate upon more in this book) as an attempt to explain the evolutionary mechanisms behind biological sociality such as altruism, aggression, and offspring nurturing. The fundamental principle guiding Wilson's sociobiology is that an organism's evolutionary success is measured by the extent to which its genes are represented in the next generation.

Elliot Sober asks, Why isn't it a matter of convention whether one describes a trait as evolving for the good of the organism or for the good of the species? He gives the answer to this question in one word: *altruism*.[129] An altruistic trait is one that is deleterious to the individual possessing it but advantageous for the group in which it is found; as such, if the organism is the exclusive unit of selection, then natural selection works *against* the evolution of altruism. However, if the *group* is a unit of selection, then natural selection—at times, anyway—*favors* altruistic traits. The important point about the units of selection problem is that there can be conflicts of interest between objects at different levels of organization: what is good for the group may not be good for the individual organism.[130]

---

127. Sober and Wilson, *Unto Others*, 17.
128. Wilson, *Sociobiology*, 3.
129. Sober, *Philosophy of Biology*, 91.
130. Sober, *Philosophy of Biology*, 91.

Part I

Seemingly altruistic bees disembowel themselves when they sting intruders to the nest; thereby they sacrifice their own lives and help the group to which they belong. Similarly, some species of crows issue warning cries when a predator approaches, which in the case of the individual crow is negative, whereas the other members of the group receive a benefit.[131] The evolutionary concept of altruism concerns the fitness effects, to self and other, of the behavior involved; thus—again seemingly—even plants and viruses can be altruistic, though they do not have minds. If organisms compete against other organisms within the confines of a single population, then natural selection will favor selfish organisms over altruistic ones, as the selfish individuals are the beneficiaries that do not incur the cost of making donations themselves. On the other hand, if groups of altruists do better than groups of selfish individuals—and individual *groups* compete against other groups—then altruism may evolve, be maintained, and perhaps even become overly advantageous and therefore prominent within the populations (ref. "higher" primate societies).

I earlier said that almost all of Darwin's many selectionist explanations deploy the concept of *individual*, not *group*, selection. And while that is true in my opinion, there are a few contexts in which Darwin forsakes an individualistic interpretation of adaptation. One of them occurs in *The Descent of Man* in his discussion of human morality. Here is Darwin's statement of the case:

> It is extremely doubtful whether the offspring of the more sympathetic and benevolent parents, or of those which were the most faithful to their comrades, would be reared in greater numbers than the children of selfish and treacherous parents of the same tribe. He who was ready to sacrifice his life, as many a savage has been, rather than betray his comrades, would often leave no offspring to inherit his noble nature. The bravest men, who were always willing to come to the front in war and who freely risked their lives for others would on average perish in larger numbers than other men.[132]

131. Cf. Sober, *Philosophy of Biology*, 91.
132. Darwin, *The Descent of Man*, 1: 163.

The Secular Evolutionary Worldview (SEW) Defined & Explicated

So, then, we are left with a quandary: if altruistic self-sacrifice is deleterious for the individual, though good for the group, how can it evolve? Darwin responds to this question, quasi-directly:

> It must not be forgotten that although a high standard of morality gives but a slight or no advantage to each individual man and his children over the other men of the same tribe, yet that an advancement in the standard of morality and an increase in the number of well-endowed men will certainly give an immense advantage to one tribe over another.[133]

A third example from *The Descent of Man* is one in which Darwin discusses technological innovations that allow some human groups to outcompete others:

> Now, if some one man in a tribe, more sagacious than the others, invented a new snare or weapon, or other means of attack or defence, the plainest self-interest, without the assistance of much reasoning power, would prompt the other members to imitate him; and all would thus profit . . . If the new invention were an important one, the tribe would increase in number, spread, and supplant other tribes.[134]

So, then, Darwin's discussion of human morality requires, in the lineage leading to modern human beings, that some individuals embraced an altruistic morality while others did not. This variation in phenotype may have been due to genetic differences between individuals, but Darwin's hypothesis is also consistent with a moral inclination to altruistic behavior evolving by cultural group selection.[135] Perhaps the traits are transmitted from one generation to the next by teaching and learning, not by genes.[136] Indeed, for Darwin and the Darwinian lineage, relatedness is the condition under which altruism evolves under the influence of group selection; it is not a condition that cancels the operation of group selection.

---

133. Darwin, *The Descent of Man*, 1: 163.
134. Darwin, *The Descent of Man*, 1: 161.
135. Cf. Boyd and Richerson, *Culture and the Evolutionary Process*.
136. Sober, *Did Darwin Write the Origin Backwards?*, 62.

Part I

3

The God of Chance

An Elucidation of Chance in (Macro-)Evolution

THE ROLES THAT THE concept of chance plays in understanding the world around us have changed dramatically over the centuries. For example, for many Enlightenment thinkers, chance was at best an admission of ignorance. Consider Voltaire, who quite forcefully said, "'Chance' is a word void of sense; nothing can exist without a cause."[1] In Darwin's *On the Origin of Species*, we still see traces of this sentiment in statements like this: "I have hitherto sometimes spoken as if the variations . . . had been due to chance. This, of course, is a wholly incorrect expression, but it serves to acknowledge plainly our ignorance of the cause of each particular variation."[2] This quote, however, stands against dozens of other uses of chance in *On the Origin of Species* that seem to imply the illuminating power of chance. Darwin, it seems, then, was inconsistent in usages of the term "chance."

Indeed, Darwin uses the term "chance" sixty-seven times in *On the Origin of Species*, and most of these instances are in the

---

1. Voltaire, *Mélanges de Philosophie*, 26.
2. Darwin, *On the Origin of Species*, 131.

Part I

context of either the origin of variation—for example, he writes: "the chance of their appearance will be much increased by a large number of individuals being kept"[3]—or survival and reproduction: "the best chance of surviving and of procreating their kind."[4] In some places, even, Darwin seems to endow "chance" with causal powers of its own, as when he states: "Mere chance, as we may call it, might cause one variety to differ in some character from its parents."[5] He elsewhere steadfastly denies such a causal version of "chance."

We thus see in Darwin a great tension—one that derives from his unique position as one of the—if not the—last great scientific thinkers who worked exclusively prior to a profound shift in our understanding and use of chance, probability, and (later) statistics. What occurred in the subsequent decades in evolutionary biology is a fascinating transition from chance as a placeholder for unknown mechanisms, something to be replaced with deeper understanding, to chance taking a central explanatory role.[6] This "probabilistic revolution" or "taming of chance," as it has variously been described by commentators, came late for Darwin, who—for example—owned, but never used, the seminal works of Adolphe Quetelet, who was the first person to extensively develop the use of statistics in science.[7] Statistics were later seized upon, however, around the turn of the twentieth century by a group of biologists who wished to transform the life sciences into a veritable mathematical science.[8] By the time these early-twentieth-century biologists were done and their work was taken up by the modern synthesis, biology then and forever more became a statistical science.

However, it is increasingly likely that randomness does *affect* the course of evolution, though just how much is a disputed question. For Stephen Jay Gould, it dominates (macro-)evolution and

3. Darwin, *On the Origin of Species*, 41.
4. Darwin, *On the Origin of Species*, 81.
5. Darwin, *On the Origin of Species*, 111.
6. Cf. Hacking, *The Taming of Chance*; Krüger et al., *Ideas in History*; and Krüger et al., *Ideas in the Sciences*.
7. Cf. Quetelet, *Sur l'homme et le développement de ses facultés*.
8. Cf. Pence, "The Early History of Chance in Evolution," 48–58.

The God of Chance

with it the larger history of life.⁹ This oft-told story of the development of chance in evolutionary theory, as the contributors to *Chance in Evolution* make clear, is at best overly simplified. For one reason, the history of chance in evolution does not begin with Darwin, nor does it end with the formulation of the modern synthesis. This is because the idea that the natural world is "chancy" by no means spontaneously generated in the late nineteenth century. It may be contextualized, rather, within a debate that spans several of the most important figures in the history of philosophy, from Democritus through Aristotle, Aquinas, and Kant, up to the present day.¹⁰

Insights from *Chance in Evolution*¹¹

As the numerous chapters within *Chance in Evolution* on contemporary biology make plainly clear, the "chancy" nature of evolution by no means forms a static and settled picture. All contributors to *Chance in Evolution*, of which there are twelve, agree that it is now nearly impossible to discuss contemporary evolutionary theory in any depth without making reference to at least some concept of "chance" or "randomness": many processes are described as chancy, outcomes are characterized as random, and many evolutionary phenomena are thought to be best described by stochastic (or probabilistic models). Chance, in fact, is taken by the twelve authors in *Chance in Evolution* to be central to the understanding of fitness, genetic drift, macroevolution, mutation, foraging theory, and environmental variation, for example. The full impact of chance, however—as pointed out by the authors—is only beginning to be fully understood. This is a history—that is, the status, frequency, and the persistence of chance in (macro-)evolution—to which more is added every proverbial day in the contemporary era.

---

9. Cf. Gould, *Wonderful Life*; Blount, "History's Windings in a Flask," 244–63; and Erwin "*Wonderful Life* Revisited," 277–98.
10. Ramsey and Pence, "Chance in Evolution from Darwin to Contemporary Biology," 2.
11. Cf. Ramsey and Pence, *Chance in Evolution*.

Part I

For example, beyond the question of whether particular biological phenomena should be considered chancy, there is a major challenge in understanding what is basically meant by "chance": what conceptually, as well as empirically, does it mean to ascribe "chance" to a particular process or a specific outcome? After all, various writers may intend a wide variety of different things when they use terms like "chance," "randomness," or "stochasticity." So, then, in order to get a handle on this diversity of meanings, Ramsey and Pence, in their introduction to *Chance in Evolution*, begin by drawing a few broad distinctions. First, they contend, a person might be making reference to a particular sequence of outcomes, claiming that this sequence is random, in the sense often deployed by mathematicians. Randomness, then, in this sense, is a property of outcomes, such as a large number of flips of a fair coin.

Second, scholars who use these terms might be speaking about a subjective sense of unpredictability, describing the inability (ignorance) of a particular agent to make a certain prediction within the context of a particular theory. Notably, Plutynski et al. in their chapter in *Chance in Evolution* describe this sense of chance as a "proxy for probability."[12] Third, scholars could consider events to be "chancy" in the sense of being unusual or unlucky for a particular kind of organism within a particular environment or selective regime. Finally, in a fourth sense, scholars might be speaking either of a variety of indeterminism that arises, *sui generis*, at the level of evolutionary theory, or of indeterminism in evolutionary theory connected to or based on indeterminism in other areas of science, such as physics.

These four senses, of course, Ramsey and Pence immediately instruct us, by no means exhaust the philosophical distinctions that can be drawn among concepts of "chance."[13] Each of these notions is grounded in a particular trajectory in the history of philosophy and the history of biology and has inspired a variety of responses throughout science and culture. This dizzying multiplicity of ways of understanding chance should humble us all. It definitely does me.

12. Plutynski et al., "Chance in the Modern Synthesis," 77.
13. Ramsey and Pence, "Chance in Evolution from Darwin to Contemporary Biology," 3.

The God of Chance

Also in *Chance in Evolution*, David J. Depew chronicles the history of the idea of contingency in biology. Contingency, he argues, has been a hallmark of biology since the time of Aristotle. There were, to be sure, some countervailing influences arising under the rubric that Ernst Mayr later called "essentialism" or "Platonism."[14] These come, however, not from Plato, but from the seventeenth-century botanical community, and they must be weighed against a long-standing focus in the life sciences on contingency and the similar-but-not-identical relationship between parents and offspring. Genuine indeterminacy, too, is an old idea, looming in the background of debates over the life sciences in the figure of Epicurus. According to Ramsey and Pence, then, the contemporary prominence of chance should thus be seen less as an historical aberration than as an attempt to understand, formalize, and quantify chance in its many manifestations, dating back to the earliest speculation on the sciences of life.[15]

In his chapter,[16] Depew develops these points by tracing a series of shifting alignments since antiquity among the closely related, overlapping, but distinguishable concepts of contingency, chance, and randomness. These alignments affect how biological teleology—the ascription of functions, end-directedness, and adaptedness—is conceived and how it relates to natural selection. Depew makes six main points:

1. The history of biological contingency is much older than Darwin. In fact, there are elements of contingency even in Aristotle's theory of generation and, since contingency is the opposite of necessity, in his concept of hypothetical necessity.[17]
2. Species fixism of the sort that figures in John Dewey's, Ernst Mayr's, and David Hull's story did exist, but it isn't nearly as ancient as they imply. It arose, instead, in the late seventeenth

---

14. Mayr, "Typological versus Population Thinking," 26–29.

15. Ramsey and Pence, "Chance in Evolution from Darwin to Contemporary Biology," 3.

16. Cf. Depew, "Contingency, Chance, and Randomness," 15–40.

17. Cf. Lennox, *Aristotle's Philosophy of Biology*, 138–40.

century.[18] Before then, naturalists, especially botanists, were comfortable with the mutability they observed in hybrids. What changed, then, was the superimposition of the logical category of species onto biological classification and closely related efforts to involve God in fixing species boundaries.[19] Species fixism and typological essentialism, Depew concludes, are comparatively recent phenomena.

3. The idea that chance is the origin of the natural world has been around since Empedocles (ca. 490–430 BCE), Epicurus (341–270 BCE), and the Roman scientist-poet Lucretius (ca. 99–55 BCE).[20] Chance adds to contingency an element of indeterminacy, whose opposite is necessity, insomuch as whether it is located in the nature of things or only in our ignorance, defies explanation, especially explanation in terms of "purposes."

4. There was genuine novelty in Darwin's anti-Lamarckian stipulation that the causes of variation are independent of its subsequent utility in coping with environments. When variants first arise, they only happen to be useful. But if they are heritable, they can gradually evolve into adaptations by the enhanced reproductive success of the organisms that have them. Darwin uses "chance" to signify the causal independence of variation's origin from subsequent biological adaptedness.[21]

5. Darwinians were able to undercut the long-standing dichotomy between chance and purposiveness because Darwin's theorizing stood on the edge of the "probability revolution" that—by mathematically "taming" them—gave chance a key role in law-governed explanations of natural phenomena.[22] And

---

18. Wilkins, *Species*, 96.

19. Wilkins, *Species*, 89.

20. Hodge and Radick, "The Place of Darwin's Theories in the Intellectual Long Run," 248.

21. Beatty, "Chance and Design," 147.

22. Gayon, *Darwinism's Struggle for Survival*; Gayon, "Chance, Explanation, and Causation in Evolutionary Theory," 395–405; Gigerenzer et al., *The Empire of Chance*; Hacking, *The Taming of Chance*; Krüger, *Ideas in History*;

6. The discovery that the ultimate source of heritable variation is spontaneous mutation in DNA has amply justified Darwinism's postulate that variation arises independently of its subsequent adaptive utility. But this discovery has also resulted in an assimilation of chance to randomness conceived as inherent unpredictability.[23]

Darwin's own views of chance did, however, provide a truly novel approach. While chance is certainly a factor in Darwin's picture of evolution, this is chance harnessed as a positive force for the generation of adaptation. This picture of chance, nascent and not fully elaborated in Darwin's own work, sets the context for its later combination with the tools of statistics and probability at the end of the nineteenth and beginning of the twentieth centuries, as well as discoveries in genetics from the 1920s to the present, that allow biological science to recapture what Depew calls "a sense of wonder about biological purposiveness, untethered from cosmic teleology."[24] Notably, in a seminal chapter in his *Physics*, Aristotle divides chance into two sorts. The first is luck (*tuché*), which is a species of chance that because of its importance in our lives gives its name to the genus. Luck is chance in matters typically under the sway of choice, such as chancing to run into an acquaintance who owes you money that you had been meaning to recover.[25] The other species of chance is spontaneity (*to automatou*), the analogue of luck in matters under the sway of natural tendencies and impulses.[26]

In ultimately rejecting chance, Aristotle did not deny that contingency consistently crowds the etiology of living beings. The contingencies of Aristotle's embryology were buffered by his conviction that the universe is eternal, self-sustaining, and at its upper edges divine. The scope of contingency was greatly widened by Jewish, Christian, and Islamic creationism.[27] The clash between the

---

Krüger, *Ideas in the Sciences*; and Porter, *The Rise of Statistical Thinking*.

23. Depew, "Contingency, Chance, and Randomness," 17–20.
24. Depew, "Contingency, Chance, and Randomness," 35.
25. Cf. Aristotle, *Physics* II.5.197a5–6.
26. Cf. Aristotle, *Physics* II.6.197a36–b15.
27. See, for example, Hodge and Radick, "The Place of Darwin's Theories

Part I

conviction that God created the world out of nothing and the impulse of theologians to use Aristotle as a philosophical handmaiden (*ancilla*)—interestingly, Orthodox Christian theologians remained happy with neoplatonism—is an episode of such importance that the subsequent history of philosophy of biology can scarcely be understood apart from it.

Shifting from the background of chance, back to Darwin's appropriation of it, a good place to look with regard to the questions about contingency, determinism, and teleology that were philosophically at issue in the evolutionary biology of his day is to his frank correspondence with the American botanist Asa Gray, with whom he exchanged almost three hundred letters (extant) over more than three decades. Indeed, their correspondence reveals how Darwin's theory of natural selection itself continued to evolve after the appearance of *On the Origin of Species* in 1859, to embrace more contingency, more chance, and, paradoxically, more biological purposiveness.[28] Darwin—from the beginning—greatly appreciated Gray because he understood natural selection better than most early readers of *On the Origin of Species*. Gray knew, for example, that "without the competing multitude no struggle for life; and without this, no natural selection and survival of the fittest, no continuous adaptation to changing circumstances, no diversification and improvement."[29] Thus, Darwin relied heavily on his American pen-pal to help him tear asunder both a hostile and misinformed interpretation of natural selection that began circulating in the United States almost immediately after the original publication of *On the Origin of Species* in 1859.

Through his long correspondence with Gray, Darwin began to recognize the implications of his discoveries for envisioning how chance variation is related to adaptive natural selection.[30] Increas-

in the Intellectual Long Run," 252.

28. For a detailed account of the Darwin-Gray correspondence, see: Lennox, "The Darwin/Gray Correspondence 1857–1869." For an accounting of its politically charged context, see Moore, "Darwin's Progress and the Problem of Slavery," 555–82.

29. Gray, *Darwiniana*, 378.

30. For this point, reference Lennox, "The Darwin/Gray Correspondence

The God of Chance

ingly, he thought that although heritable variations are small, continuous, and ubiquitous, their opportune occurrence is not part of any equilibrating mechanism, making them more fortuitous than he had earlier believed; even when they happen to be available, moreover, there exists no more than an enhanced chance that organisms fortunate enough to possess them will survive, reproduce, and pass on their advantages to descendants.[31] His exchange with Gray, in fact, pushed Darwin even further in this direction. He recognized that, to be effective, natural selection must give chance its freedom to dance about without restriction. Thus liberated from the pull of natural theology that still had residue within his psyche, Darwin's most basic idea became *agnostic* in tendency. Notably, this weasel word had just been coined by Thomas Henry Huxley.

So, then, Darwin's beliefs moved in an opposite direction from the one toward which Gray had hoped to nudge him. While this leaves unaddressed the question of evolutionary progress (teleology writ large) within the bounds of Darwinian principles, it seems to me to be a reckoning point in Darwin's views of the same.[32] Even though contemporary humans may not be the preset goal of the evolutionary process, they are, however—at least from a biological perspective—an *ex post facto* result of natural selection's tendency to favor cognitively powerful species as less complex niches—occupied by less complex entities—become unavailable. After all, the distinguished mid-twentieth-century population geneticist Theodosius Dobzhansky argued that cognition flourishes in culturally mediated niches.[33]

An intensification of the escalation of chance, as opposed to what may be called intelligent design, whether direct or indirect by way of created laws, was not the only effect of Darwin's encounter

1857–1869," as well as Lennox, "Darwin and Teleology," 152–57.

31. Depew, "Contingency, Chance, and Randomness," 30.

32. For a variety of views on "progress," see Richards, *The Meaning of Evolution*; Ruse, *Monad to Man*; Ruse, "Does Darwinian Evolution Mean We Are Here by Chance?," 122–42; Moore, "Darwin's Progress and the Problem of Slavery," 555–82; along with my own forthcoming book entitled *Macroevolution, Contingency, & Uncontrolling, Amoreopotent Love*, particularly chapter 3.

33. Cf. Dobzhansky and Boesiger, *Human Culture*.

Part I

with Gray. In the course of responding to a shockingly misplaced and errant reading that mistook natural selection for nothing more than chance plus time, Darwin came to realize that since the process of natural selection is necessarily gradual—working continuously over many generations on a virtual plethora of minutely differing and fortuitously available variations—its heritable effects spread because of the adaptedness of the resulting condition. Even relative adaptedness builds on earlier successes and so results in very beautiful "contrivances," as Darwin frequently called them. The carefully observed work of Darwin's later years—especially on insect-devouring plants,[34] orchids,[35] and earthworms[36]—is *more* adaptationist than *On the Origin of Species* itself.[37] Indeed, the adapted traits of these particular species presuppose a world full of contingencies, shot through, that is, with chance and unguided toward any direction in particular.

But, these adapted traits and the organisms that functionally integrate them are not at all like the contraptions cobbled together by various primitive theories of evolution, for natural selection pictures them as gradually spreading through populations because of their amplification of good effects for their possessors. So, then, while significantly different from Aristotle's teleological understanding of evolution, Darwin's adapted organisms nevertheless also "come to be and to exist for the sake of" the life activities they promote.[38] For Depew, Darwin's growing appreciation of the role of chance in the process of adaptive natural selection had two conceptual consequences. For example, the conjunction of chance and selection stimulated his enhanced appreciation of the exquisitely

---

34. Cf. Darwin, *Insectivorous Plants*.

35. Cf. Darwin, *On the Various Contrivances by which British and Foreign Orchids are Fertilised by Insects*.

36. Cf. Darwin, *The Formation of Vegetable Mould*.

37. For this point, see Lennox, "Darwin *Was* a Teleologist," 409–21; Lennox, "Teleology by Another Name," 493–95; and Beatty, "Chance Variation," 629–41.

38. For this point, see Depew, "Incidentally Final Causation and Spontaneous Generation," 285–97; and Depew, "Accident, Adaptation, and Teleology," 116–43.

functional nature of the "contrivances" they combined to evolve. In this sense, and in this sense alone, Darwin really was a (biological) teleologist.[39] Second, the chancy relation between variation and selection also implies that chance means no less and no more than the contingent nature of reproductively beneficial consonance between heritable variation, environmental utility, and natural selection.[40]

There is no guarantee, however—or even presumption—that appropriate variation will be available. Regarding this point, Darwin wrote to Gray, "I cannot think that the world as we see it is the result of chance, and yet I cannot look at each separate thing as the result of design . . . I am in a hopeless muddle."[41] In another letter he told Gray, "I am inclined to look at everything as resulting from designed laws, with the details, whether good or bad, left to the working out of what we may call chance. Not that this notion at all satisfies me."[42]

Notably, two continuity theses are defended in Jonathon Hodge's article[43] in *Chance in Evolution*: 1) that there was no radical shift in Darwin's thinking about chance and chances when, late in 1838, he first formulated his theory of natural selection; and 2) that the theory, construed by Darwin as a probabilistic and causal theory, has not changed since into a noncausal, statistical theory. Darwin's views, in great and illuminating detail, provide the material for Jonathan Hodge's contribution referenced here. Hodge deeply penetrates into Darwin's work in his early notebooks, with Hodge arguing that Darwin's views on the nature of chance—despite occasional claims to the contrary—remained largely consistent and constant, and were not greatly altered by his first formulation of the theory of natural selection in 1838. Darwin is wholly committed, Hodge argues, to the metaphysical position that we would now call determinism, and to the understanding of chance as nothing

---

39. For this assertion, see Lennox, "Darwin *Was* a Teleologist," 409–21; Lennox, "Teleology by Another Name," 493–95, and Lennox, "Darwin and Teleology," 152–57.

40. Depew, "Contingency, Chance, and Randomness," 31.

41. Darwin, "Letter 2998."

42. Darwin, "Letter 2814."

43. Cf. Hodge, "Chance and Chances in Darwin's Early Theorizing," 41–75.

more than our ignorance of the precise details of biological systems. The central focus of these invocations of chance is, and remains throughout Darwin's published works, the reference to natural selection as a process that, while chancy, is not what Hodge calls "fortuitous"[44]—for it is for a very well-determined reason that the fitter organisms survive while the less fit perish.

In a highly provocative conclusion, Hodge expands his claims about Darwin's works to the realm of contemporary philosophy of biology. For just as a causal process of non-fortuitous differential reproduction was central to Darwin's picture of natural selection, Hodge argues, we have received no evidence in the intervening years since 1838 that would lead us to interpret natural selection, and the chance that we find therein, in any other way. In so doing, he invokes two clusters of issues, which will be laid out in what follows.

First, Darwin constructed his theory as a theory of probabilistic causation, not as a theory of forces, but by combining a concept of chance as accident with a concept of chances as probabilities. Chance hereditary variations are ultimately directly due to causal accidents, and some of these chance, one-off variations cause higher chances of survival and reproduction in the individuals varying in accordance with the variation. Because the accidental advantageous chance variations have the causal effects they do, it is no accident that their own chances—and their own probabilities—of survival and reproduction are higher than those who are unvaried. Any such probable differential survival and reproduction may then be called non-fortuitous, because concepts of the accidental and of the fortuitous often coincide. Second, Darwin clarified this naturally non-fortuitous causation by comparing and contrasting it with the non-fortuitous causation at work in artificial selection. Even today, biologists continue to do likewise, for better or for worse.[45]

Moving forward from the Darwinian period specifically, the thinkers of the modern synthesis are the subject of the chapter entitled "Chance in the Modern Synthesis," also in *Chance in Evolution*,

---

44. Hodge, "Chance and Chances in Darwin's Early Theorizing," 58.
45. Hodge, "Chance and Chances in Darwin's Early Theorizing," 71.

The God of Chance

by Anya Plutynski et al.[46] Despite a widespread acknowledgment that the role of chance in evolution shifted dramatically during this period of consolidation of Darwin's ideas into a promotable theory, described as the modern synthesis, no comprehensive study of the ways the key authors from that period understand chance has yet been prepared. Until now, that is. Plutynski and colleagues seek to explicate the role of chance and its various cognates with the Darwinian understanding of evolution by natural selection that was integrated with the Mendelian or genetic picture of heredity and breeding in the modern synthesis.

Indeed, in examining the central works of Ronald A. Fisher,[47] Sewall Wright,[48] Theodosius Dobzhansky,[49] Ernst Mayr,[50] George Gaylord Simpson,[51] and G. Ledyard Stebbins,[52] Plutynski and colleagues describe and track five separate notions of chance through a pivotal period in the history of biology, spanning some two decades from the 1930s to the 1950s. They conclude that, while these authors certainly found much about which to disagree, a core set of five meanings for chance is rather much held in common by the aforementioned authors. This core set of five meanings for chance are expressed in a fairly widely shared set of evolutionary processes, including mutation, meiosis, geographic isolation, inbreeding, genetic drift, and even microscale indeterminism and macroscale contingency.

So, then, according to Plutynski and colleagues, the changes in the modern synthesis do not represent a conceptual shift in how chance is understood, or even a transformation in views about where chance appears in evolution. Rather, these changes in the modern synthesis regard the relative importance attributed—as an empirical matter of fact—to each of the various notions of chance

---

46. Cf. Plutynski et al., "Chance in the Modern Synthesis," 76–102.
47. Cf. Fisher, *The Genetical Theory of Natural Selection*.
48. Cf. Wright, "Evolution in Mendelian Populations," 97–159.
49. Cf. Dobzhansky, *Genetics and the Origin of Species*.
50. Cf. Mayr, *Systematics and the Origin of Species*.
51. Cf. Simpson, *Tempo and Mode in Evolution*.
52. Cf. Stebbins, *Variation and Evolution in Plants*.

Part I

in evolutionary processes. Indeed, the modern synthesis in evolutionary biology is taken to be that period in which a consensus developed among biologists about the major causes of evolution, a consensus that informed research in evolutionary biology for at least a half-century.

As such, it is a particularly fruitful period to consider when reflecting on the meaning and role of chance in evolutionary explanation.[53] Biologists of this period make reference to "chance" and loose cognates of "chance," such as "random," "contingent," "accidental," "haphazard," or "stochastic." Of course, what an author might mean by "chance" in any specific context varies. Notably, the name "modern synthesis" was coined by Julian Huxley in 1942, whose book *Evolution: The Modern Synthesis*[54] was both a comprehensive overview of then-current biology and an articulation of a research program. The theoretical work and organizational events of the modern synthesis spanned roughly three decades, from circa 1920 to 1950.[55]

This "modern synthesis" period exhibited a marked fluctuation of views about the role(s) of chance in evolution, eventuating in a "hardening,"[56] or emphasis on selection that continued well past the synthesis period. The stabilization of the modern synthesis's view on chance (insomuch as there was a stable view) was established firmly in the 1940s, with the major texts of this period all significantly drawing upon the population genetic documents published during the "early phase" of the modern synthesis, primarily accomplished by Haldane, Fisher, and Wright in the 1920s and 1930s.[57] Significant further work was done in the 1940s through the 1950s, which made clear the extremely close relationships of ecology to evolution and of paleontology to systematics.

As aforementioned, according to Plutynski et al., there were (at least) five different senses of chance at play in the modern

53. Plutynski et al., "Chance in the Modern Synthesis," 76.
54. Cf. Huxley, *Evolution*.
55. Plutynski et al., "Chance in the Modern Synthesis," 78.
56. Gould, "The Hardening of the Modern Synthesis," 71–93.
57. Plutynski et al., "Chance in the Modern Synthesis," 78.

The God of Chance

synthesis.[58] First, one might assume appeals to chance in science to be making metaphysical claims about the world as fundamentally indeterministic; only rarely, however, is the question of determinism or indeterminism addressed overtly during the modern synthesis. Theodosius Dobzhansky[59] and J. B. S. Haldane[60] wrote works toward the end of their careers that approached philosophical issues such as free will and indeterminism, and interest in such questions was apparently a lifelong passion in the case of Sewall Wright.[61] However, through 1950, when appealing to chance and its various cognates, most modern synthesis authors were silent about "quantum indeterminacy." Indeterminism in physics indeed did play an important role for R. A. Fisher,[62] but in most cases the modern synthesists, when discussing chance, are referring to events and processes at a more macro-scale: that is, the segregation of genes, the isolation of small subpopulations of animals, and so forth.

Second, Plutynski et al. contend that the term "chance" is sometimes used interchangeably with "random."[63] There are more and less precise senses of "random," it should be noted; the most precise sense is the notion of a random variable. Random sampling from a uniform distribution results in outcomes that are equiprobable, meaning equally probable, whereas sampling from nonuniform distributions results in outcomes that are not equiprobable. When speaking of random mating or random sampling of alleles in the process of meiosis, most modern synthesis authors appear to be referring to a sampling process of which outcomes are assumed to be equiprobable. That is, given the limited understanding of the structure of the gene and the causes of mutation at the molecular and submolecular levels at the time, the authors of the modern

---

58. Plutynski et al., "Chance in the Modern Synthesis," 79.

59. Cf. Dobzhansky, *The Biological Basis of Human Freedom*; Dobzhansky, *Mankind Evolving*; and Dobzhansky, *The Biology of Ultimate Concern*.

60. Cf. Haldane, *New Paths in Genetics*.

61. Cf. Provine, *Sewall Wright and Evolutionary Biology*.

62. Fisher, "Indeterminism and Natural Selection," 99–117.

63. Plutynski et al., "Chance in the Modern Synthesis," 79–80.

synthesis indeed meant that they were unsure about the relevance of quantum indeterminacy.[64]

Third, and most often, Plutynski et al. assert, chance is used as a proxy for probability.[65] For instance, possession of a single trait might raise (or lower) the chances of some fortuitous outcome. All modern synthesis authors speak of natural selection as a matter of probabilities, or as probabilistic in the sense that even exceptionally high fitness does not guarantee survival or reproductive success, but only increases an organism's "chances" of survival. Likewise, the chance (probability) that a random gene combination is adaptive was thought to be low.[66] The chances of various outcomes are thus spoken of as "high" or "low," when outcomes are unequally probable.

Fourth, Plutynski et al. note that events such as floods, storms, meteorites crashing into the earth, and volcanoes are sometimes spoken of by modern synthesis authors as chance, random, or contingent events. Such events are "chancy" in the sense that they are rare and they result in (usually) non-fortuitous outcomes for organisms, lineages, and species, which are unusual, "unlucky" (or not predictable), given existing biogeography, survivorship, or ongoing ecological circumstances; volcanic explosions, mutations, lightning strikes, and other random events in this sense are uncorrelated with other causes that shape evolution (e.g., selection).[67] In other words, such events inherently disrupt current trends by dividing landscapes, wiping out resources, or eliminating (or isolating) groups of species that would otherwise be interbreeding.

Fifth, and finally, according to Plutynski et al., chance is often used to refer to outcomes in contradistinction to or "opposing" selection. Remarkably, Sewall Wright speaks of both drift and mutation as "chance" factors that "oppose" selection.[68] This is probably due to the fact that the outcomes of drift and mutation are random,

---

64. For a contrary view, see Sloan and Fogel, *Creating a Physical Biology*.
65. Plutynski et al., "Chance in the Modern Synthesis," 80.
66. Cf. Wright, "The Roles of Mutation," 358.
67. Plutynski et al., "Chance in the Modern Synthesis," 80–81.
68. Wright, "The Roles of Mutation," 359.

in the second sense defined by Plutynski et al., described above. Indeed, for a particular trait and environment, selection will have a predictable "direction," whereas drift and mutation result in outcomes that are relatively unpredictable. Such chance outcomes are not "directed," be it toward some desired (adaptive) outcome, or toward (really) any outcome in particular. After all, most modern synthesis authors assumed that mutations were usually deleterious. So, then, what synthesis authors meant by "chance" in any particular instance was context-dependent, insomuch as a chance event was often defined in terms of a contrast, with a "directional" cause, process, or tendency, or a predicted outcome.[69]

A distinctive Darwinian view of the natural world emerged from the modern synthesis. What this Darwinian view amounted to was subject to various nuances, but all agreed on what Stephen Jay Gould later called the "fundamental principles of Darwinian central logic"[70]: that selection acts by and large on individual organisms, that selection leads to both genetic changes in populations through (micro-)evolution and speciation through (macro-)evolution, and that the very same causes of evolution in populations were responsible for the divergence of species and lineages. Moreover, all saw themselves as responding to various "opponents" to this "Darwinian" view, including anti-evolutionists, as well as "orthogenicists" and neo-Lamarckians. The core commitments of many of the modern synthesis authors, according to Plutynski et al., included at least the following:[71]

1. First, they saw their work as providing a "Darwinian" alternative to "directed" or "orthogenetic" views of evolution, according to which evolution has a predetermined direction.
2. Second, they held that the origin (mutation) and sorting (recombination) of genes are in some sense chance or random processes.
3. Third, they all viewed natural selection as a probabilistic cause of adaptive change in populations. And

69. Plutynski et al., "Chance in the Modern Synthesis," 82.
70. Gould, *The Structure of Evolutionary Theory*, 19.
71. Plutynski et al., "Chance in the Modern Synthesis," 91.

4. Fourth, they all took the current distribution of species and adaptations as, in large part, a matter of contingency, both in terms of when and where mutations arise and are sorted in meiosis, and in terms of which environmental challenges are presented, that is, whether "contingent" events like storms, floods, and natural disasters were more or less in operation in the ecology and evolution of any lineage.

While it is clear that none of the modern synthesists agreed on every minute detail, they nevertheless all agreed, in way or another, on the following six points:[72]

1. Mutation is the ultimate source of variation, and mutations arise "by chance," where this is understood as by and large to be of deleterious effect (or, that is, not "directed" toward adaptation).
2. Meiosis is a source of "random" variation (in sexual reproduction) in that there is a 50/50 chance of receiving alleles—that is, one of two or more alternative forms of a gene that arise by mutation and are found at the same place on a chromosome—from either of two chromosomes, that is, from one's maternal or paternal stock.
3. Isolation of small subpopulations is a source of "random" variation, in the sense that peripheral isolates in many cases may be treated as "random" samples from parent populations.
4. Inbreeding is a source of chance gene combinations; that is, isolation of small (and thus genetically unique) subpopulations can be a source of evolutionary novelty.
5. While it is unknown what the causes of mutation are at the submolecular level, the role of radiation in inducing mutation suggests, but does not prove, that indeterminism may play a fundamental role in evolutionary change. And
6. Contingent events play a significant role in macroevolutionary change—for example, due to catastrophic events such as geological and/or climatological changes, yielding extinctions,

---

72. Cf. Plutynski et al., "Chance in the Modern Synthesis," 98; this list is only slightly modified by me.

The God of Chance

isolation of species and genera, and/or variable rates of (macro-)evolutionary change.

In sum, the modern synthesis authors shared a set of core commitments about the role(s) of "chance" in evolution. They agreed that chance plays an important explanatory role in evolution and that appeals to chance are not simply an acknowledgment of ignorance. Rather, appeals to chance (and its cognates) were to be interpreted as proxies for appeals to probability, random sampling, contingent events, or events in contrast to natural selection.

In Douglas H. Erwin's article in *Chance in Evolution*, entitled "*Wonderful Life* Revisited: Chance and Contingency in the Ediacaran-Cambrian Radiation,"[73] he notes the historical development and current best understanding of the fossils of the Burgess Shale. It is these fossils that led Stephen Jay Gould, in his 1989 *Wonderful Life*,[74] to argue for an extremely powerful role for contingency in the history of life. The years since the publication of Gould's work, however, have not been silent. They have produced manifold fossil discoveries, revisions to a variety of phylogenetic relationships, and theoretical and conceptual models that have changed our understanding of (macro)evolution. So, then, as a logical extension, the appraisal of these important fossils must change as well.

Gould famously argued that any "replay of the tape of life" would result in the evolution of dramatically different forms, thereby making historical contingency one of the most powerful forces in evolution. Erwin reconsiders this argument in light of an extensive and expertly surveyed catalog of Ediacaran-Cambrian radiation research in the past two and a half decades. Erwin stipulates that enhanced methods have made the "strange" fauna of this period less so, elucidating (some of) their connections to known stem groups, but also confirming—at the same time—Gould's emphasis on the impressive changes in morphology that took place during this period. Tests of the contingency hypothesis itself, including the Long-Term Experimental Evolution (LTEE) Project directed by Richard Lenski at Michigan State University since 1988,

73. Cf. Erwin, "*Wonderful Life* Revisited," 277–98.
74. Cf. Gould, *Wonderful Life*.

Part I

and studies of convergent evolution (e.g., Simon Conway Morris[75] and George R. McGhee[76]), combined with a classification of five different types of contingency, enable Erwin to evaluate the status of Gould's argument.

Indeed, Erwin makes the following classificatory organization of five types (or senses) of contingency:[77]

1. Drift or sampling error, which Gould explicitly rejected as a form of contingency, although not always to the satisfaction of other scholars.[78]
2. Unpredictability, in which the outcome of a process cannot be determined from a prior state of affairs.[79]
3. Causal dependence, or sensitivity to initial conditions, in which a prior state is necessary to reach a particular outcome.[80] Derek Turner, in fact, suggests that contingency as causal insufficiency might be a better term for this concept.[81] John H. Beatty even argued that although unpredictability and causal dependence can be complementary, Gould ultimately failed to distinguish between them and often, in fact, conflated the two.[82]
4. Sensitivity to external disturbance, which is related to the resilience of a historical process and is distinct from sensitivity to initial conditions.[83] And

---

75. For Simon Conway Morris's writings on this topic, see Conway Morris, *The Crucible of Creation*; Conway Morris, *Life's Solution*; Conway Morris, "The Predictability of Evolution"; and Conway Morris, "Evolution: Like Any Other Science It Is Predictable," 133–45.

76. Cf. McGhee, *Convergent Evolution*.

77. Erwin, "*Wonderful Life* Revisited," 290.

78. See, e.g., Beatty, "Replaying Life's Tape," 345; Travisano et al., "Experimental Tests," 87–90.

79. Beatty, "Replaying Life's Tape," 345.

80. See Beatty, "Replaying Life's Tape," 346; see also Ben-Menahem, "Historical Contingency," 99–107; and Ben-Menahem, "Historical Necessity and Contingency," 120–30.

81. Turner, "Gould's Replay Revisited," 65–79.

82. Beatty, "Replaying Life's Tape," 336–39.

83. Inkpen and Turner, "The Topography of Historical Contingency," 1–19.

5. (Macro-)evolutionary stochasticity, which centers upon unbiased species sorting. Derek Turner, in a discussion of Beatty's theses, suggested that Gould's argument in *Wonderful Life* is largely focused on (macro-)evolutionary sorting among species, and that Gould viewed contingency as an issue of unbiased species sorting, rather than the sampling error problem in point 1 above. Turner claimed: "Evolutionary contingency is the random or unbiased sorting of entire lineages. It *just is* the macroevolutionary analogue of random drift."[84]

We have, in short, a mixed bag—the status of Gould's contingency hypothesis depends dramatically on three things: 1) the evidence at issue; 2) the variety of contingency under discussion; and 3) the level of evolutionary process of interest, whether it be molecular, developmental, phenotypic, or (macro-)evolutionary.[85]

Insights from *The Challenge of Chance*[86]

As Klaas Landsman, Ellen van Wolde and Noortje ter Berg note in *The Challenge of Chance*, the "collapse of cohesion is one of the features that characterize chance."[87] By sheer accident, or so it seems, something breaks the typical regularity of the natural world, and the ensuing feelings of uncertainty and apprehensiveness, in turn, trigger us humans to search for explanations that will help restore order and normal patterns of cause and effect. In a word, according to the authors, we are challenged by chance, and we have been so at least since antiquity, if not before. So, then, how do we contemporary humans respond to such challenges wrought by the presence of chance in the natural world?

For thousands of years people have tried to decide whether chance is a fundamental and irreducible phenomenon—that is, certain events are not caused, but they just happen—or whether

---

84. Turner, "Gould's Replay Revisited," 69; emphasis in original.
85. Erwin, "*Wonderful Life* Revisited," 278.
86. Cf. Landsman and van Wolde, *The Challenge of Chance*.
87. Landsman et al., "Introduction," 1.

chance is merely a reflection of our ignorance. Either way, we contemporary humans find the experience of chance hard to deal with. Humans incessantly try to understand random phenomena and prefer explanations that (re)install meaning to the events that they struggle with brought on, as it were, by chance. The question, then, is whether this search for explanation and meaning has succeeded, or—at least!—has a fighting chance to succeed.

From Aristotle to the eighteenth century, natural philosophy had seen the patterns within the natural world as real, with our (human) role being limited to discovering them. From Hume and Kant onwards, however, the causal patterns that permeate traditional science began to be questioned. Moreover, with his revolutionary claim that the universe is necessarily the way it is and yet has no goal, Benedict Spinoza cut the thread connecting explanation and purpose. This thread connecting chance and explanation was thereafter challenged by Darwin's theory of evolution in the nineteenth century, followed by the promulgation of quantum theory in the twentieth, in both of which chance plays a fundamental role in explanation. In the twentieth century, however, it seems that causality is claimed to be a mere by-product of our subjective need for rules, patterns, and meaning, which eventually led Bertrand Russell to his famous witticism about causality:

> All philosophers, of every school, imagine that causation is one of the fundamental axioms or postulates of science, yet, oddly enough, in advanced sciences such as gravitational astronomy, the word "cause" never appears ... To me, it seems that ... the reason why physics has ceased to look for causes is that, in fact, there are no such things. The law of causality, I believe, like much that passes muster among philosophers, is a relic of a bygone age, surviving, like the monarchy, only because it is erroneously supposed to do no harm.[88]

Christoph H. Lüthy and Carla Rita Palmerino, in "Conceptual and Historical Reflections on Chance (and Related Concepts)," contend that in everyday language, the use of such words as "chance,"

---

88. Russell, "On the Notion of Cause," 1.

The God of Chance

"coincidence," "luck," "fortune," or "randomness" strongly overlap.[89] In fact, in some languages, such as German, they coincide in one word (*Zufall*). In other languages, there is a clear separation between chance events with positive connotations (e.g., "luck," "fortune") and those with bad ones (e.g., "accident," "hazard"). In their contribution to *The Challenge of Chance*, they try to sketch the main lines of development of several of these concepts from the ancient Greeks up to modern times—or more precisely—from Democritus and Aristotle up to the world of quantum mechanics. Three elements, they claim, emerge with particular force.

First, "chance," "fortune," "randomness," etc. are in some instances invoked as explanations of events, while in others these terms designate events that occur without an explanation(s). Second, the meaning of these terms only becomes clear when one understands which alternatives they exclude. Third, it is conspicuous to see how, after a rigid exclusion of "chance" or "randomness" from the domain of scientific explanation in the early modern period, they were restored to full glory in nineteenth- and twentieth-century biology.

Most ordinary people would probably agree with the Enlightenment philosopher David Hume that "'chance,' when strictly examined, is a mere negative word, and means not any real power which has anywhere a being in nature."[90] One important reason why it is impossible to give a coherent account of this negative word and of its siblings is that they are used both to offer an explanation and to signal the lack of an explanation. Indeed, depending on the context, "chance," "coincidence," "randomness," or "luck" do not only indicate the presence or absence of a recognizable causal logic, but they also indicate unknown probabilities, which might or might not be calculable.[91] Despite the elusive and contradictory explanatory value of this cluster of words, there are some interesting things than can be said about them. Indeed, Lüthy and Palmerino first

---

89. Lüthy and Palmerino, "Conceptual and Historical Reflections on Chance," 9.

90. Hume, *An Enquiry Concerning Human Understanding* 8.1.

91. Lüthy and Palmerino, "Conceptual and Historical Reflections on Chance," 10.

Part I

employ an etymological approach to understanding these words, followed by a more general historical approach to the same.

Lüthy and Palmerino, in fact, in some detail survey a number of key moments in the history of scientific (or natural philosophical) thought, from the divine fate of Greek tragedy and the chance swerve of Epicurean atoms through the deterministic machine world *a la* Descartes up to the reintroduction of chance and randomness in scientific theories as diverse as evolutionary theory and quantum physics. In this section, they contend that, as a general rule, philosophy and science have repeatedly tried to drive chance and coincidence out of their domain—unless they could stand for a precise type of causal factor that was required for a specific type of physical explanation—but that, time and again, chance entered anew through the "back door."[92]

Lüthy and Palmerino stipulate that "*cadere*," the Latin verb for "to fall," stands in fact at the root of several of the words that they investigate in this chapter within *The Challenge of Chance*. To begin with, there is the Latin noun, "*casus*"—"the fall"—a word that can describe the falling of snow, but also everything else that literally "befalls" humans, however improbable it may be. *Casus* is therefore also the Latin word for "chance," "coincidence," or "luck." The word "coincidence" also derives from the Latin verb *cadere*, but in a more readily visible way. A "coincidence" takes place when things "fall (*cadere*) together." The word is not ancient Latin, but medieval instead, and it seems to have first been used in astrology, where "*coincidentia*" referred to the joint influence of multiple planets. This genealogy of the term "coincidence" gives one an indication of a basic difference between "chance" and "coincidence": the latter requires more than one thing to happen at the same time. So, then, in the sentence, "By chance, I was born into a rich family," the term "coincidence" would not fit in its stead. That said, in the sentence: "By coincidence, I happened to meet Philip Clayton at a Regent University colloquium in 2008, and I enrolled at his graduate school in 2018," is an appropriate usage of the term "coincidence."

---

92. Lüthy and Palmerino, "Conceptual and Historical Reflections on Chance," 11.

The God of Chance

Lüthy and Palmerino then turn to an examination of a number of key moments in the intellectual—that is, philosophical and scientific—evolution that our words have undergone, and the explanatory (or causal) role that was attributed or denied to them. They start with ancient Greece, because it is there that our current terminology takes its origin. It is also there that one finds, for the first time in Western intellectual history, a debate about the status of unexpected events and the way that humans must deal with them conceptually. In ancient Greece, the word that designated an unexpected turn of events in a human life or in the observed natural world was "*tuchê*." In Greek comedies, tragedies and in works of historiography, *tuchê* is invoked to designate unforeseen events, which may derive from the gods or from mere fortune.

Aristotle's most extensive treatment of chance is found in book 2 of his *Physics*. As is often the case, Aristotle starts his analysis with a historical excursus. Previous philosophers have failed to give an account of chance, he tells us, which is all the more surprising as some of them have attributed to chance a fundamental role in their physical systems.[93] Aristotle thinks of, for example, Empedocles's cosmogony, which relies on air that moves upwards by chance and speaks of the haphazard origin of limbs of animals. Aristotle thinks even more of Democritus, who maintains that "the cosmic order came by chance . . . whereas neither animals nor plants are, or come to be, by chance, but are all caused by Nature or Mind or what else." Aristotle laughs at this idea, arguing,

> But if this really were so, that very fact ought to give us pause and convince us that the matter needs investigation. For, in addition to the inherently paradoxical nature of such an assertion, we may note that it is exactly in the movements of the heavenly bodies that we never observe what we call casual or accidental variations, whereas in all that these people tell us is exempt from chance such things are common. Of course, it ought to be just the other way.[94]

---

93. Aristotle, *Physics* 2:195b30–196b9.
94. Aristotle, *Physics* 2:196a25–196b5.

Part I

Aristotle inverts the order: for him, "regular and customary successions," such as those observed in the heavenly motions, must happen by necessity, whereas the terrestrial realm is defined by a great degree of randomness. Regular necessity is observed throughout the superlunary sphere, where the sun, the planets, and the stars are located and which is defined by one single element, ether, and by constant, circular movements. By contrast, in the sublunary sphere, where the four elements constantly mix and unmix, objects continuously come about and perish again. Here, where we find irregularity and surprising events, we may truly speak of products of chance.

Aristotle admits that, in our sublunary domain of permanent change, "what we call luck or chance corresponds to some reality."[95] At the same time, he rejects the suggestion that *tuchê* should be viewed as a specific type of causality. Instead, chance events should be regarded as accidental, that is to say, concomitant effects of a definite cause: *Tuchê*, Aristotle writes in his *Physics*, "is a cause only accidentally."[96] But what does it mean to be an accidental cause? In his *Metaphysics*, Aristotle defines "accident" as that which happens "neither necessarily, nor usually," adding that there is "no definite cause for an accident, but only a chance, i.e., indefinite cause."[97]

So, then, if a man goes to the market and "accidentally" meets his debtor, "the reason of his meeting him was that the wanted to go marketing; and so too in all other cases when we allege chance as the cause, there is always some other cause to be found."[98] The man may have wanted to buy cheese and vegetables, but, "as it happened," he encountered his debtor. That the verb "*sumbainô*," of which "*symbebêkos*" ("accident") is the past participle, literally means "to walk together," is most suitable for this specific Aristotelian example, as it provides a quite visual model for what I earlier defined as a "coincidence": two men walking, each steered by his own intentions, to the market, but "accidentally" end up in each other's company.

---

95. Aristotle, *Physics* 2:196b15–17.
96. Aristotle, *Physics* 2:197a14f.
97. Aristotle, *Metaphysics* 1:1025a15.
98. Aristotle, *Physics* 2:196a1–8.

The God of Chance

In order to make sense of Aristotle's distinctions, one has to remember that his entire universe, and the causality that is active in it, is everywhere purposeful and goal-driven, so that the explanations he offers tend to be teleological. In such a universe, *tuchê* is an "accident" in the sense that it designates those events that eschew all purposes. In the natural world, a typical class of "accidents" is constituted by monstrous births, which may be regarded as "failures of purpose in Nature"[99] in the sense that accidental factors hindered the natural development of the seed. Being "characteristic of the perishable things of the earth,"[100] chance manifests itself above all in the domains of biology and of human actions.

In the domain of natural history—what would later become biology and geology—the eighteenth century ushered in a more chaotic worldview. God receded from his previous role as the designing creator as well as the guarantor of an all-pervasive necessity, as our world gradually turned out to have a tempestuous past made of ice ages, inundations, volcanic eruptions, extinct species and ultimately of forms of life that diversified in unpredictable ways in reaction to these circumstances. Indeed, an impressive and ever-increasing battery of eminent authors emerged who would deny the distinction between a contingent realm of human actions and a deterministic realm of nature.

One may observe, beginning in the eighteenth century, an increasing insistence on the accidental nature of all forms of life, including mankind. Julien Offray de La Mettrie, in his famous *L'Homme machine*, provocatively stated that human existence had been thrown upon the Earth at hazard, "just like mushrooms," mushrooms being at the time in many quarters still seen as imperfect beings that were generated spontaneously.[101] And as biologists began to get an inkling of the changing morphology of species, they arrived at the concomitant idea of "innumerable multitude of individuals" produced by "chance" (hazard) and of "fortuitous combinations of

---

99. Aristotle, *Physics* 2:199b4.
100. Aristotle, *Parts of Animals* 641b15.
101. de La Mettrie, "L'homme machine," 1:46.

the productions of nature," of which the species living today are only "a small part of what blind fate has produced."[102]

The epitome of that trend is of course Charles Darwin's *On the Origin of Species* of 1859,[103] which introduces the notion of a blind natural selection, and which relies on a very simple combination of factors: there is a random type of variation of traits found among siblings (a longer or shorter neck, thicker or thinner fur, greater or lesser need of water, etc.); a deadly struggle for survival due to the presence of predators, a perennial excess of offspring, and the resulting scarcity of food and resources; as well as the resulting selection of those randomly generated traits that happen to give their owners an advantage in the struggle for survival. These traits, selected again and again across numerous generations, would eventually lead to such modifications in a population that a new species or even genus could come about. Importantly, there existed, for Darwin, no underlying evolutionary direction or logic. The environmental factors were as accidental as the traits they selected among the randomly generated variants. Whether a thicker fur happened to be an advantage or a disadvantage for survival depended on changing weather patterns, diseases, the presence of predators and many other unpredictable conditions.

C. S. Lewis mocked this vision of nature in the first lines of his satirical "Evolutionary Hymn":

> Lead us, Evolution, lead us
> Up the future's endless stair;
> Chop us, change us, prod us, weed us.
> For stagnation is despair:
> Groping, guessing, yet progressing,
> Lead us nobody knows where.[104]

Lewis parodies here a famous hymn by James Edmeston (1821), which to this day is found in all Anglican and Episcopalian hymnals and whose first verses read as follows:

---

102. de Maupertuis, "Essai de cosmologie," 1 1–58.
103. Cf. Darwin, *On the Origin of Species*.
104. Lewis, *Poems*, 55.

The God of Chance

> Lead us, heavenly Father, lead us
> o'er the world's tempestuous sea;
> guard us, guide us, keep us, feed us,
> for we have no help but thee;
> yet possessing every blessing,
> if our God our Father be.

Notably, the lack of providentialism is clearly expressed in Darwin's model:

> In such case, every slight modification, which in the course of ages chanced to arise, and which in any way favoured the individuals of any of the species, by better adapting them to their altered conditions, would tend to be preserved; and natural selection would thus have free scope for the work of improvement.[105]

Darwin honestly admitted that he had no idea about the forces that were responsible for the variability of traits found in offspring. After all, the (re-)discovery of Mendelian genetics and the discovery of DNA were later episodes in the history of biology. Nevertheless, his basic model has remained fairly intact, as has the role of chance in it. For example, modern biology speaks of the role of mutations in the evolution of species in terms of spontaneous mutations or mutations due to errors occurring in the replication of DNA. The default process is faithful copying, but errors take place by the *ad hoc* collocation of atoms, which are unexplained deviations from the usual direction.

In the eyes of the American philosopher, logician, chemist, and mathematician Charles Sanders Peirce, Darwin's evolutionary theory in fact constituted strong evidence against a deterministic worldview. As soon as he read Darwin's *On the Origin of Species*, Peirce—who was one of the first people in the United States to understand statistical mechanics—immediately grasped what was eluding Darwin and his circle. He went on to sketch an evolutionary theory based on assigning more reality to the path-dependent workings of contingency and chance in the fabric of the universe

---

105. Darwin, *On the Origin of Species*, 82.

than Darwin did.[106] Quite generally, Peirce combated the idea that the universe was governed by strict laws, preferring to see mathematical laws of nature as nothing more than statistical approximations to general patterns or "habits," as he called them, which natural bodies tended to exhibit. In fact, taking recourse to the Greek word *tuchê*, Peirce coined in 1892 the neologism "tychism" as the name of the view that the universe was characterized by "absolute chance" and not by a deterministic type of "necessity." Peirce thereby dismissed the idea "that every single fact in the universe is precisely determined by law."[107] That mistaken idea had been around since the days of Democritus and the Stoics, but after the seventeenth century, it began to be clad in new scientific clothes, looking thus: "Given the state of the universe in the original nebula, and given the laws of mechanics, a sufficiently powerful mind could deduce from these data the precise form of every curlicue of every letter I am now writing."[108]

But—Peirce retorted—the so-called "laws of mechanics," like all laws of nature, are mere "approximations." The more exact one's experimental measurements, the greater the deviations of the data from the mathematical ideal. In the essay's concluding dialogue between an imaginary determinist and Peirce, which starts with a discussion over whether the apparently random fall of a die is determined or not, the real force of tychism is finally introduced. In an evolving cosmos, which displayed ever-increasing complexity over time, all apparent mechanical regularity could at best be provisional. In other words, one had to admit "pure spontaneity or life as a character of the universe, acting always and everywhere though restrained within narrow bounds by law, producing infinitesimal departures from law continually, and great ones with infinite infrequency."[109]

Given the developments in evolutionary biology and quantum physics over the past 150-plus years, it seems rather as if "chance,"

---

106. Peirce, "Evolutionary Love," 176–200.
107. Peirce, "The Doctrine of Necessity Examined," 321.
108. Peirce, "The Doctrine of Necessity Examined," 323.
109. Peirce, "The Doctrine of Necessity Examined," 333–34.

"randomness," and "coincidence" have been restored to a place of respectability that they had previously lost. Heraclitus, the Greek philosopher, once famously said, "Everything changes and nothing remains still; you cannot step twice into the same stream," stressing the ever-changing nature of reality. Randomness and chance are inherent to scientific methodology and theory. Indeed, whether our personal surprise at a given event is merely a sign of personal ignorance or is instead a necessary feature of this universe has once again been elevated to the status of an unresolved question. In a fitting close for this chapter, I will quote the famous physicist Erwin Schrödinger, who once wrote,

> By the laws of physics we are forced in each moment to do whatever we do. What is the point then in considering whether it is right or wrong? Where is there any room for a moral law, if the omnipotent law of nature does not provide it with a chance to speak? Today, the antinomy is as unresolved as it was twenty-three centuries ago.[110]

---

110. Schrödinger, *Expanding Universes*, 18.

PART II

The God of Chance and Purpose—Theological Assists by Philip Clayton and Alister McGrath

4

The God of Contemporary Science

Dialoguing with Clayton

PHILIP CLAYTON'S GOAL IN *God and Contemporary Science* is to examine the doctrines of God, of God's relation to the world, and of God's activity in the world.[1] How can one take scientific results seriously and still engage in theological inquiry?, Clayton asks rhetorically. Clayton defends the theses that metaphysical and theological issues are raised by the methods and conclusions of science; this endeavor may require revisions to dearly-held theological conclusions, but theologians must be intellectually honest with the data. Although evolution may be compatible with theology in terms of divine "purpose," it does not follow that evolution gives credence to notions of such a purpose, as in the old understanding of natural theology.[2]

In this work, Clayton asserts that two of the most important questions today in theology are God's relation to the world and his mode of activity (if at all) within it.[3] Believers must think of God as an agent whose involvements are consistent with the nature that one ascribes to him. In fact, Clayton suggests that

1. Clayton, *God and Contemporary Science*, 6.
2. Clayton, *God and Contemporary Science*, 8.
3. Clayton, *God and Contemporary Science*, 9.

Part II

we should follow [Jürgen] Moltmann's interpretation of continuous creation, namely as a type of divine creation that is not contingent upon God's direct action, but upon the processes established and parts of nature that are already created.[4]

Moltmann writes,

> If we are trying to find a new interpretation of the Christian doctrine of creation in light of the knowledge of nature made accessible to us by evolutionary theories, we must distinguish more clearly than did the traditional doctrine of creation between creation in the beginning, continuous creation, and the consummation of creation in the kingdom of glory.[5]

Moltmann is perhaps the most forceful recent proponent of the doctrine that holds that God indwells within his "creation":

> By the title, "God in creation," I mean God the Holy Spirit. God is "the lover of life" and his Spirit is *in* all creative beings . . . This doctrine of creation, that is to say, takes as its starting point the indwelling divine Spirit of creation . . . the creator, through his Spirit, *dwells* in his creation as a whole, and in every individual creative being, by virtue of his Spirit holding them together and keeping them in life.[6]

It seems to me, then, that a God whose Spirit is so closely identified with creation needs to be affected, and even altered, by what happens in it. It might also seem a natural development to think of God as suffering along with his creation, as has often been observed: "An immanent creator cannot but be regarded as creating through such a process *and so as suffering in, with and under it.*"[7]

As theologian/scientists, the textual accounts of Yahweh as creator in Genesis 1 must be read as pseudo-scientific accounts of

---

4. Clayton, *God and Contemporary Science*, 23–24.

5. Moltmann, *God in Creation*, 206.

6. Moltmann, *God in Creation*, xiv.

7. Brümmer, *Interpreting the Universe as Creation*, 112. Emphasis in the original.

The God of Contemporary Science

the world.[8] In fact, "creation is neither myth (in the common sense of fiction) nor a historical account in the way in which historical records are generally written (*Historie*). It is 'prehistory.'"[9] Yahweh, who drew the world up out of chaos, does not leave it in chaos; notably, however, Genesis 1:1 does not require *creatio ex nihilo* (although that is, ultimately, what Clayton himself favors).[10] Genesis is first and foremost a description of God's creative and redemptive acts: it reveals to us that God's actions as "creator" are both past and present.[11] *Creatio continua*, then, is both providence and sustenance, as God's creative activity is extended; that God uses "the other" to create is consistent with the biblical understanding of providence—creation recapitulates redemption.[12] Clayton further notes the assertion that God has used the "instrumentality of humans to achieve his plans is basic to the biblical understanding of Providence. Why then challenge whether he could use natural laws of physical processes—either before or after the advent of humanity—to achieve the divine plan?"[13]

In fact, Clayton contends that the traditional creation doctrine of *creatio ex nihilo* arose as a present-tense doctrine, one which was less concerned with the initial act of God than about the ongoing dependence of the created order upon God.[14] For Clayton, the import of the doctrine of creation for theology cannot be overstated, because it deals with the universality of the Israelite claims regarding its God. The God-who-saves is first of all the God-who-creates.[15] The creation account, then, *forces* universal significance. Philosophical and systematic theologians cannot but deal with the sciences, therefore.[16]

---

8. Clayton, *God and Contemporary Science*, 17.
9. Clayton, *God and Contemporary Science*, 68.
10. Clayton, *God and Contemporary Science*, 20.
11. Clayton, *God and Contemporary Science*, 22.
12. Clayton, *God and Contemporary Science*, 22–25.
13. Clayton, *God and Contemporary Science*, 24.
14. Clayton, *God and Contemporary Science*, 26.
15. Clayton, *God and Contemporary Science*, 50.
16. Clayton, *God and Contemporary Science*, 57.

Part II

Clayton stipulates that two of the most urgent problems raised for theology by modern science include the problems of how to conceive of God's relation to the world and how, if at all, to conceive of God's agency in the world.[17] The work of the Spirit mediates between the Father and the Son, completing the Son's work on earth, notes Clayton,[18] which is direly important—I contend!—for a view of divine involvement and activity in the (late-)modern world. Indeed, Clayton concedes that it may be better to view "innerworldly causality" as a manifestation of divine agency, which is why panentheism and divine activity are closely linked, as panentheism seems to suggest that there is no qualitative difference between the regularity of natural law and the intentionality of divine activities.[19] The "conceptual disciplines" of natural theology, philosophical theology, and metaphysics contribute many postulations to a theology of the God/world relation.[20] For example:

- They provide general conceptual criteria for the doctrine of God, which are formal standards for the doctrine; that is:
    1. They must be coherent.
    2. They must be adequately comprehensive.
    3. They must have explanatory power.
- They provide models of God that can be filled with theological content.
- They provide a distinct picture of what occurs when theological motifs are thought about systematically.
- They allow us to formulate the alternatives to Christian theology in a rigorous manner (e.g., panentheism). And
- They turn our attention back to the universality of the claims made by the Scriptures.

---

17. Clayton, *God and Contemporary Science*, 9.
18. Clayton, *God and Contemporary Science*, 60.
19. Clayton, *God and Contemporary Science*, 100–01.
20. Clayton, *God and Contemporary Science*, 115–119.

The God of Contemporary Science

Panentheism is better able, Clayton notes, to address the problem of divine agency in our contemporary scientific and philosophical context.[21] For Clayton, God—who contains the universe as a whole (though he is much more than it as well)—can act directly on the universe as it is constrained, in and through the overarching context.[22] In *God in Creation*, Moltmann notably "shows convincingly why a full understanding of creation must eventually lead theologians to something like panentheism, the position which he himself advocates, and not to pantheism in the sense that the defenders of orthodoxy feared."[23] In Moltmann's presentation, what plays the key role is reflection on the question of "God's relationship to space and time"—is that there really are "separately existing things, which means that they are spread out in real space and time."[24] As Moltmann notes, "If space is interpreted as the dimension of God's omnipresence, pantheistic conclusions are impossible."[25] God can, after all, only be present to all parts of his creation if there really are such parts in the first place.[26]

Moving on to consideration of Big Bang cosmology and theology, naturalism, and causality, Clayton then offers eight theses which suggest how scientific discoveries "plead for meta-physical, and ultimately theological, treatment and interpretation."[27] In fact, Clayton summarizes the implications of contemporary cosmological research by noting:[28]

1. God's time is not our time.
2. God created the heavens and the earth with a Big Bang.
3. The universe reveals mathematic, lawlike behavior.
4. This universe was possible, if not probable, to emerge from the "beginning."

---

21. Clayton, *God and Contemporary Science*, 119.
22. Clayton, *God and Contemporary Science*, 223.
23. Clayton, *God and Contemporary Science*, 88.
24. Clayton, *God and Contemporary Science*, 88.
25. Moltmann, *God in Creation*, 154.
26. Cf. Clayton, *God and Contemporary Science*, 89.
27. Clayton, *God and Contemporary Science*, 161.
28. Clayton, *God and Contemporary Science*, 158–60.

Part II

5. This universe appears to be designed in order for humanity to inhabit it on earth.
6. Theology must assume and posit that everything works together for the good (Rom 8:28), even the incalculable suffering caused through evolution.
7. Theology can make assertions about humanity that cannot be derived from science. And
8. Theology can make assertions about the future that cannot be derived from science.

From this data set, Clayton concludes that theism in general, and panentheism in particular, is best able to integrate scientific results with what we know about human existence in the world.[29] Perhaps more than anything else, the discussion between science and religion today concerns the overriding presumption of ontological naturalism; nomological science, unparalleled in its ability to explain phenomena in the world, however, does not rule out divine activity in the world.[30] In fact, the integration of science and theology is a subject of theology proper.[31]

Clayton then goes on to distinguish three kinds of divine intervention:

1. General conservation or sustaining (not at odds with natural science, note, because it is trans-empirical);
2. Psychological interventions (miracles); and
3. Physical interventions in the natural world.

The latter kind raises the toughest problem, for if we are to have a full theory, theology must give an account of "where the causal joint is at which God's action directly impacts on the world."[32] Without such a theory, theologians would fail to make sense of their own views. They would also fail in their apologetic task, for on any strong naturalist reading, divine agency in the world is physically impossible. As Clayton notes, God need not be defined

---

29. Clayton, *God and Contemporary Science*, 160.
30. Clayton, *God and Contemporary Science*, 171–73.
31. Clayton, *God and Contemporary Science*, 189.
32. Clayton, *God and Contemporary Science*, 192.

The God of Contemporary Science

as spirit in opposition to the world (ontological dualism) as long as matter is not seen as evil or inferior . . . if humans are really made in the image of God, imbreathed [sic] with the God-given spirit, then it would be more natural to conceive of God as Spirit working in and through at least some parts of the material world.[33]

This is but one reason why I, in the notions advocated in this present title, do *not* posit a causal joint, but leave the notion of divine involvement in an evolutionary world ambiguous, nebulous, and indefinite. In fact, this is why I generally propose divine involvement and activity from the *future*, not from the past or present. In my understanding, the Spirit precedes the universe, transcends it, but also could be said to be manifested within it, which is panentheism to the core. I agree with Clayton, who notes that a "complete account of divine agency would have to include a top-down component."[34] In view of such, and in fact in response to Clayton, I aver that my view of divine involvement in an evolutionary world, which I have putatively coined as "spirit-derived causation" (SDC), provides *explanatory adequacy*, some sort of *causal agency*, and *ontological homogeneity*, for "to be real is to have causal powers."[35]

Clayton makes an impressive argument for panentheism as the preferable way to conceive of the relation between God and the world: "We are not God because we are different in our fundamental nature from God . . . The world is contained within God; yet the world is not identical to God."[36] Going yet further, Clayton notes in support of panentheism that it

> turns out to be impossible to conceive of God as fully infinite if it is limited by something outside of himself. The infinite may without contradiction include within itself things that are by nature finite, but it may not stand *outside* of the finite. For if something finite exists, and if

---

33. Clayton, *God and Contemporary Science*, 98.
34. Clayton, *God and Contemporary Science*, 247.
35. Kim, "Downward Causation," 135.
36. Clayton, *God and Contemporary Science*, 90.

the event is "excluded" by the finite, then it is not truly infinite or without limit.[37]

To put this into my own terms, it seems that Clayton is stating that there is simply no place for finite things "outside" of that which is *absolutely unlimited*. Thus, it is by necessity that an infinite God encompasses the finite natural world, thereby directly making it in some sense "within" Godself, which is the conclusion that theologians refer to as panentheism.

Moreover, for Clayton, the issue of divine causality explains why panentheism and a theory of divine involvement are so closely linked together. He asserts that the involvement of God can be much more coherently conceived when "the world bears a relationship to God analogous to the body's relation to mind or soul."[38] This is what Clayton calls the "Panentheistic analogy."[39] So, then, for Clayton, this panentheistic analogy suggests that

> there is no *qualitative* or ontological difference between the regularity of natural law and the intentionality of special divine actions. Put differently, it would seem to deny that only the latter should count as divine actions and not the former. Instead, natural laws, when viewed theologically, will count as descriptions of the predictable regularity of patterns of divine action.[40]

After a careful response to the challenge of naturalism, Clayton turns to the theme of divine causality in nature in light of the natural sciences. He states,

> The question is not how to prove that God is active in the world at particular moments, but rather how to think this possibility in a manner that does not conflict with what we now know of the world (through science).[41]

---

37. Clayton, *God and Contemporary Science*, 99.
38. Clayton, *God and Contemporary Science*, 100.
39. Clayton, *God and Contemporary Science*, 101.
40. Clayton, *God and Contemporary Science*, 101.
41. Clayton, *God and Contemporary Science*, 193.

The God of Contemporary Science

This leads Clayton to discuss areas in science which might provide evidence for a radical openness (i.e., "ontological indeterminacy") in nature which would allow for divine causality in specific events. Two such areas (and their supporters) assume a "bottom-up" approach to divine action: chaos theory (John Polkinghorne) and quantum mechanics (Thomas Tracy, Nancey Murphy, and Robert Russell). Arthur Peacocke, instead, urges a "top-down" approach in which God acts on the "world as a whole." Clayton carefully analyzes each of these approaches and concludes that Peacocke's work comes closest to a (his?) panentheistic theory of divine causality.[42] He then combines top-down and bottom-up approaches to divine causality using such philosophical concepts as emergence and supervenience. Clayton makes a powerful argument for

> a theory of God as divine agent which is both a product of theological reflection and consistent with (and perhaps even suggested by) what science has come to know about the natural world and the place of human agents within it. According to the panentheism I have defended, God can act on any part of the world in a way similar to our action on our bodies. At the same time, God also transcends the world and will exist long after the physical universe has ceased.[43]

So, then, for Clayton, the *"single greatest positive result of current discussions in cosmology lies in the fact that scientific results plead for meta-physical, and ultimately theological, treatment and interpretation."*[44] This assertion of Clayton's leads, logically, to the next chapter of this book.[45]

---

42. Cf. my forthcoming volume: McCall, *The Peacocke's Tale*.
43. Clayton, *God and Contemporary Science*, 264.
44. Clayton, *God and Contemporary Science*, 160–61. Emphasis in original.
45. For more of Clayton's infinitely valuable insights, please my own edited volume: McCall, *God and Gravity*.

5

A (Renewed) Natural Theology

Dialoguing with McGrath

ACCORDING TO EMIL BRUNNER, it is the task of our theological generation to "find its way back to a proper natural theology."[1] He argues that, since God "leaves the imprint of his nature upon what he does," it follows that it is fundamentally a Christian belief that the "creation of the world is at the same time a revelation, a self-communication of God."[2] It is relevant to my argument in this chapter that Brunner here does not consider his natural theology as *proof* of God, but rather as consistent with belief in God. Natural theology, fortunately, is enjoying a renaissance, catalyzed both by the intellectual inquisitiveness of natural scientists and the reflections of Christian theologians. Natural theology can be broadly understood as the systematic exploration of a proposed link between the everyday world of our experience and another asserted transcendent reality, an ancient and pervasive idea that achieved significant elaboration in the thought of the early Christian fathers.[3]

Natural theology offers, for example, an important conceptual framework for the exploration of Christian theology as a rational

1. Brunner, "Natur und Gnade," 375.
2. Brunner, "Natur und Gnade," 343.
3. McGrath, *The Open Secret*, 2.

A (Renewed) Natural Theology

enterprise and a clarification of how the Christian faith relates to scientific postulates. Natural theology mandates a principled engagement with reality that is theologically and scientifically informed. It has the potential to open up new vistas of understanding between scientific and religious cultures. There remains, however, a widespread perception that Charles Darwin's theory of natural selection marked and continues to mark the end of any viable natural theology, particularly in its classic formulation. But I shall argue in this chapter that there is a "wider natural theology" that remains untouched by Darwinian formulations of evolution by natural selection. It is my intention to provide the basic outlines of a workable natural theology from below that is in dialogue with the biological sciences, particularly the theory of evolution by natural selection.

In *Summa theologica* I.2.3, Aquinas argues that the "existence of God can be proved in five ways." Aquinas's fifth way, for example,

> is taken from the governance of the world. We see that things which lack intelligence, such as natural bodies, act for an end, and this is evident from their acting always, or nearly always, in the same way, so as to obtain the best result. Hence it is plain that not fortuitously, but designedly, do they achieve their end. Now whatever lacks intelligence cannot move towards an end, unless it be directed by some being endowed with knowledge and intelligence; as the arrow is shot to its mark by the archer. Therefore some intelligent being exists by whom all natural things are directed to their end; and this being we call God.[4]

Aquinas's fifth way hinges on the Aristotelian understanding of final causality. In such a view, it is believed that efficient causation, such as A causing B, cannot be understood except in light of final causation, that is, that there is a natural end in A that causes it to produce B. For if in A there was no inherent end towards B, it would be impossible to account for why A is always or nearly always the efficient cause for B, rather than C or D. Thus B acts as

---

4. Aquinas, *Summa Theologica* I.2.3.

Part II

a final cause for A. It is on this understanding of causal regularities that exist in nature that Aquinas formulates his proof.

In *Aquinas*, Edward Feser states that

> a struck match generates fire and heat rather than frost and cold; an acorn grows into an oak rather than a rosebush or a dog; the moon goes around the earth in a smooth elliptical orbit rather than zigzagging erratically; the heart pumps blood continuously and doesn't stop and start several times a day; condensation results in precipitation which results in collection which results in evaporation which in turn results in condensation and so forth.

Feser goes on, noting that in each of these cases there are regularities that

> point to ends or goals usually totally unconscious, which are built into nature and can be known through observation to be there whether or not it ever occurs to anyone to ask how they got there. In particular, one can know that there are these ends, goals, purposes in nature whether or not it ever occurs to anyone to consider the purposes, or even the existence, of a designer of nature.[5]

The idea of teleology originates in Aristotle's discussion of natural generation, and in this discussion, he argues that explanatory priority must be given to what lies at the end of the process, that is, its goal (*telos*). For Aristotle, *telos* designated an apparent internalized goal, not the purpose of an external agent.[6] Francisco J. Ayala, an evolutionary biologist, notes,

> A teleological explanation implies that the system under consideration is directively organized. For that reason, teleological explanations are appropriate in biology ... Moreover, and most importantly, teleological explanations imply that the end result is the explanatory reason for the *existence* of the object or process which serves or leads to it ... the use of teleological

---

5. Feser, *Aquinas: A Beginner's Guide*, 116.
6. McGrath, *Darwinism and the Divine*, 189.

A (Renewed) Natural Theology

explanations in biology is not only acceptable but indeed indispensable.[7]

I take issue with Aquinas's attempt to *prove* the existence of God by his fifth way, that of teleology, as per his statement directly to that effect in *Summa Theologica* I.2.3. I say this because one cannot demonstratively prove the existence of God through reference to teleology. Rather, the congruence of such a position with the existence of God can be read from the interpretation of nature. In contradistinction to Aquinas and in dialogue with Alister McGrath, I posit that natural theology can be pictured as the process of *seeing* nature from the perspective of a Trinitarian ontology.[8] Indeed, it is commonly said that the world at which the theologian looks and the world at which the secularist looks are one and the same. In fact, nature can be *read* in theist, atheist, or agnostic ways. McGrath agrees. Also a scientist by training, McGrath seeks to open conversations, redirect thinking, explore new options, and lay the groundwork for a renewed vision of *Christian* natural theology. In so doing, he constructs a three-part argument, which will be highlighted in what follows.

McGrath characterizes natural theology as the systematic exploration of a proposed link between the everyday world of our experience and an asserted transcendent reality.[9] He broadly argues that if nature is to disclose the transcendent, it must be read in certain—i.e., specific—ways. Instead of continuing with the notoriously ambiguous, conceptually fluid, and imprecise traditional definition of natural theology, McGrath proposes a distinctively Christian approach to natural theology. He argues that a Christian view of it provides the interpretive framework by which nature can be *seen* to connect with the transcendent, thus picturing natural theology as an enterprise of *discernment*. He argues against the view of natural theology as designating an argument directly from the observation of nature to demonstrate the existence of God, a view which was popularized in the Enlightenment and formalized

---

7. Ayala, "Teleological Explanations in Evolutionary Biology," 12.
8. McGrath, *Darwinism and the Divine*, 201.
9. McGrath, *The Open Secret*, 2.

Part II

by William P. Alston[10] in the twentieth century. Rather, a Christian natural theology points to the God of the Christian faith, and not some abstract deity. In this, McGrath agrees with Hauerwas, who maintains that "the God who moves the sun and the stars is the same God who was incarnate in Jesus of Nazareth."[11]

McGrath's *The Open Secret* Explored More Fully

Part 1 of McGrath's *The Open Secret* considers the perennial human interest in what is perceived to be the transcendent. In spite of everything, we continue to speak about God in the contemporary culture, which attests to the divine's status as an important and meaningful concept. He illustrates the concept's persistence in supposed secular times, describing the methods and techniques that have been used to depict the significance and value of humanity along the way. McGrath discusses three recent examples of thinking about the transcendent: Iris Murdoch's Platonic perspective,[12] Roy Bhaskar's critical realist perspective,[13] and John Dewey's pragmatic perspective.[14] He then highlights four ways to encounter the transcendent, seemingly arguing for a conflation of the second and fourth models: 1) ascending from nature to the transcendent; 2) seeing through nature to the transcendent; 3) withdrawing from nature into the human interior; and 4) discerning the transcendent within nature.[15]

The second part of *The Open Secret* moves beyond the general quest and sets the search for transcendence within in a particularly

10. Cf. Alston, *Divine Nature and Human Language*.

11. Hauerwas, *With the Grain of the Universe*, 15–16.

12. Murdoch, *The Sovereignty of Good*, 91. See also the more extended discussion in Murdoch, *Metaphysics as a Guide to Morals*.

13. See, for example, Collier, *Critical Realism*. McGrath makes extensive, though not uncritical, use of this concept of critical realism throughout his scientific theology project; see especially McGrath, *Reality*, 195–244. For an assessment of McGrath's usage of Roy Bhaskar, see Shipway, "The Theological Application of Bhaskar's Stratified Reality," 191–203.

14. For further discussion on Dewey's pragmatic perspective, see Sleeper, *The Necessity of Pragmatism*.

15. See chapter 4 of McGrath, *The Open Secret*, 59–79.

A (Renewed) Natural Theology

Christian context in three lucid chapters. In chapter 6, for example, he elaborates on the notion that nature is not merely neutral, but actually *ambiguous*, as God is one who *hides* himself (Isa 45:15). However, that God chose to inhabit the material order affirms that it has the *capability* to reveal the divine. Herein, he depicts natural theology as an engagement with nature resting on a trinitarian and incarnational ontology. The next chapter, 7, includes a detailed exploration of the historical origins and flaws of several families of natural theology that arose in response to the influence of the Enlightenment and thereafter continued well into the twentieth century. In response to his explorations of past depictions of natural theology in chapter 7, McGrath sets forth his Christian approach to natural theology in chapter 8. He asserts that nature has the capacity to be a conduit of the divine.[16]

Part 3 of *The Open Secret* is McGrath's more constructive addition to the discussion of natural theology, offering suggestions to expand the concept of natural theology as well as its possibilities for engagement with the (late-)modern world. He re-conceives natural theology to involve every aspect of the human encounter with nature—its rational, imaginative, and moral dimensions. In chapter 9, McGrath invokes the so-called Platonic triad of truth, beauty, and goodness as a heuristic framework for his proposed natural theology, reinterpreted in a Christian manner, allowing him a distinctly Christian way of beholding, envisaging, and appreciating the natural order. The tenth chapter explores the place of sense-making for a natural theology, affirming its significance, yet denying that it can "prove" the existence of God. Chapter 11 uses the category of beauty to explore the affective engagement with nature and how that perspective can be incorporated into a revised natural theology.

All in all, McGrath largely argues that nature is an indeterminate concept, that natural theology is an inescapably empirical discipline, that a Christian natural theology concerns the *Christian* God, and that a natural theology is incarnational, not dualist. Nature is herein seen to be an "open secret" in that it is a publicly accessed entity although it is only truly understood from the standpoint of

---

16. McGrath, *The Open Secret*, 174.

Christian faith. As such, McGrath affirms the notion that the empirical is a legitimate means of discovering and encountering the divine. Indeed, McGrath's approach to natural theology holds that nature reinforces an existing belief in God retroactively through consonance between observation and theory.

Christian theology, for McGrath, provides an interpretative framework by which nature may be "seen" in a way that connects with the transcendent; the enterprise of natural theology is thus one of discernment—of viewing it through a particular set of spectacles, as it were—which acknowledges nature as a legitimate, but limited, conduit to the divine reality.[17] This type of natural theology holds that nature reinforces an *existing* belief in God through the resonance between observation and theory.[18] When properly understood, a renewed, defensible, natural theology represents a distinctively Christian way of viewing, beholding, envisaging, and appreciating the natural order—in ways that are not necessarily mandated by nature itself.

McGrath's Darwinism and the Divine Explored More Fully

McGrath continues a fine quasi-tradition with his title *Darwinism and the Divine: Evolutionary Thought and Natural Theology*,[19] building on what has been a prolific topic for him over the last several years: natural theology (cf. McGrath's *The Open Secret: A New Vision for Natural Theology* and *A Fine-Tuned Universe: The Quest for God in Science and Theology*). Though covering much of the same ground as his previous books on natural theology, this text is derived from his 2009 Hulsean Lectures delivered at the University of Cambridge, which marked the two hundredth anniversary of Charles Darwin's birth and the 150th anniversary of the publication of his *On the Origin of Species*. In it, McGrath, as he did somewhat

---

17. McGrath, *The Open Secret*, 3.
18. McGrath, *The Open Secret*, 5.
19. Cf. McGrath, *Darwinism and the Divine*.

A (Renewed) Natural Theology

with the aforementioned texts, examines the relation of evolutionary thought and natural theology.

In this latter title, McGrath broadly argues that nature must be *read* in certain ways if it is to disclose the transcendent. Indeed, in *Darwinism and the Divine*, McGrath defends a distinctively Christian approach to natural theology. The first part of this title seeks to clarify the multifarious meanings of both "natural theology" and "Darwinism," elucidating particularly the notion that definitions of terms are absolutely central to evaluations of relationship between terms. Part II of this title expands on the distinct form of natural theology within England during the seventeenth, eighteenth, and early nineteenth centuries; this part is largely historical in its thrust, and one might therefore think it to be inconsequential to a book that seeks to explicate the significance—in contemporary thought—of natural theology. This would be a mistaken presumption, however, as these historical chapters actually form the *core* of his argument, illustrating that today's debates over natural theology are largely overshadowed by the debates of the past: particularly this time period.

Through a careful depiction of the state of natural theology from the 1690s leading up to Paley's *Natural Theology* (1802), in *Darwinism and the Divine*, McGrath shows that numerous of the traditional judgments concerning natural theology and Darwinism cannot be sustained: for example, Darwin's writings did not (and do not) abolish the notion of teleology, merely reforming it and "widening" it (to coopt a phrase from T. H. Huxley) instead. Additionally, McGrath shows that the Bridgewater Treatises of the 1830s recognized the danger of the Paleyan approach to natural theology, at least implicitly, and therefore offered a more nuanced approach to it, in fact often accentuating the consonance (or harmony) between Christianity and the scientific exploration of nature instead of what one often interprets—wrongly or rightly—as "proofing" from the Paleyan approach to natural theology. In another important note from this section of the book, McGrath postulates and demonstrates that Karl Barth was truly criticizing this distinctly English form of natural theology, and not the generic enterprise itself.

Part II

Building from his historical treatment in the former section, part III of *Darwinism and the Divine* focuses on the contemporary situation of—at least his vision of it—natural theology, particularly with respect to the biological sciences. In sum, the overall argument of *Darwinism and the Divine* is profound in its implications: primarily, McGrath asserts that it was not the Christian enterprise of natural theology *per se* that was discredited by Darwin, but instead a specific form of natural theology that emerged in England after 1690 (often, and correctly, associated with William Paley). In lieu of the Paleyan-like natural theology, McGrath characterizes natural theology as the systematic exploration of a putative link between the everyday world of experience and a transcendent reality.

So, then, the enterprise of natural theology has, if anything, been given a new lease on life through the rise of evolutionary thought. The traditional approach to natural theology, aptly demonstrated by Aquinas, is one option among many; the rise of evolutionary thought supplemented an existing and vigorous theological critique of this approach. Natural theology needs to emerge from the shadows of this traditional approach and rediscover, retrieve, and renew alternative approaches. Natural theology cannot be understood to concern *proving* God from nature. Christians must do natural theology, rather, beholding the same realities as the general populace, and recast it as a process of "seeing" the domain of nature as affirming the resonance of what they observe with tenets of the Christian faith, without claiming that this observed resonance *proves* the truth of Christianity. After all, "the world at which the theologian looks and the world at which the secularist looks are one in the same."[20] This interpretive lens does not prove its truth; it does, however, demonstrate its utility, opening up in the process further areas of exploration and engagement.

Huxley's "Wider Teleology" Explored More Fully

Whereas deist natural theologies portrayed God as the grand designer, and Aquinas's natural theology pictured his existence as

---

20. Smith, *The Free Man*, 45.

A (Renewed) Natural Theology

provable by nature, the defensible natural theology that I argue for declares that God is attested to by the order of nature; he is signified *by*, or indicated *within*, the natural order. It is my position that the process of discerning God in nature is grounded in philosophical panentheism. In an essay from 1999, Philip Clayton defines "panentheism" as the view that the world is within God, though God is at the same time more than the world.[21] The appeal of panentheism is that the energies at work at the physical level are already divine energies, and physical regularities are already expressions of the fundamental constancy of the divine character. Thus, panentheism claims that if the world remains within and is permeated by the divine, then it is possible to speak of divine purposes being expressed even at the stage at which there are no conscious agents. The lawful behavior of the natural world, in this view, is an expression of divine intentionality.

This panentheistic position holds direct significance for a defensible natural theology for the twenty-first century, one that holds that the true meaning of nature is capable of being unlocked, but doing so requires the employment of a hermeneutical key that nature itself cannot provide. In such a view, nature attests, declares, and makes manifest the God that is *already* known by and through faith. Seen as such, faith precedes the demonstration of teleology in nature, and does not result from it—that is, it is not based on proof. It cannot be maintained that Darwin's theory caused the "abandonment of natural theology."[22] The enterprise may have been refined and redirected by Darwin's theory, but it was certainly not abandoned. Rather, Darwin's theory of evolution by natural selection demands the reform and restatement of teleology—the "wider teleology" of which T. H. Huxley spoke—not its abolition.

In fact, it could be argued that Darwin's theory opened up new possibilities for natural theology, if we take the angle that it is through evolution that God makes his creation more complex. Indeed, as Charles Kingsley, a nineteenth-century Anglican divine noted, "We knew of old that God was so wise that he could make

---

21. Clayton, "The Panentheistic Turn," 289.
22. Russett, *Darwin in America*, 43.

all things: but behold, he is so much wiser than even that, that he can make all things make themselves."[23] What impressed Thomas Henry Huxley most forcibly on his first reading of Darwin's *On the Origin of Species* was his "conviction that teleology, as commonly understood, had received its deathblow at Mr. Darwin's hands."[24] This has sometimes been misunderstood to imply that it was the notion of teleology in general which Huxley contended was discredited by Darwin, rather than a specific form of teleology. This is clearly not the case. Huxley's comments refer to teleology "as commonly understood," a veiled reference to the specific form found in classical or traditional formulations such as that of Aquinas and Paley which seeks to *prove* the existence of God. This is made clear in his 1887 lecture "On the Reception of *The Origin of Species*," in which Huxley rebutted three common criticisms of Darwin's theory of natural selection, each of which he held to be based on a misrepresentation of Darwin's views.[25]

For example, Huxley writes, "It is said that he [Darwin] supposes variations to come about 'by chance', and that the fittest survive the 'chances' of the struggle for existence, and thus 'chance' is substituted for providential design."[26] Huxley argues that this is not at all the case, and that Darwin was grossly misunderstood on this point. In fact, Darwin declared that he did not know what had caused certain things to happen, yet located these events firmly within the context of the laws of nature. Moreover, Huxley writes, "A second very common objection to Mr. Darwin's views was (and is) that they abolish teleology, and eviscerate the argument from design."[27] This view is often repeated, even in the twenty-first century, but is without merit. Huxley is quite clear that the traditional approaches to teleology, those that seek to *prove* the existence of God, face a direct challenge from Darwin's evolutionary account. However, the theory of evolution, he argues, bears witness to a

23. Kingsley, "The Natural Theology of the Future," xxvii.
24. Huxley, *Lay Sermons, Addresses, and Reviews*, 301.
25. Darwin, *The Life and Letters of Charles Darwin*, 2:179–204.
26. Darwin, *The Life and Letters of Charles Darwin*, 2:199.
27. Darwin, *The Life and Letters of Charles Darwin*, 2:201.

A (Renewed) Natural Theology

"wider teleology" that is rooted in the structure of the universe.[28] Indeed,

> the teleological and the mechanical views of nature are not, necessarily, mutually exclusive. On the contrary, the more purely a mechanist the speculator is, the more firmly does he assume a primordial molecular arrangement of which all the phenomena of the universe are the consequences, and the more completely is he thereby at the mercy of the teleologist, who can always defy him to disprove that this primordial molecular arrangement was not intended to evolve the phenomena of the universe.[29]

Ernst Mayr, similarly an evolutionary biologist, makes much the same point, arguing, "The occurrence of goal-directed processes is perhaps the most characteristic feature of the world of living systems."[30] Natural selection itself, the ultimate explanation within biology, should be considered a teleological process in that it has the net effect of increasing maximal reproductive fitness. W. D. Ross interprets *telos* as end to be the "final cause in nature," which is "a structure common to a whole *infima species*, to which individual members of the species strive *without conscious purpose* to give a fresh individual embodiment"[31] Considered in this context, therefore, it seems to be fully justified to designate the process of evolution by natural selection, as Ayala did, as teleological or end-directed.[32] This is the case because survival or reproductive success, while indeed not being the *specified* goals of living beings, can well be viewed as the end toward which they naturally tend even if without any conscious purpose. Teleological mechanisms in living organisms are biological adaptations that have arisen as a result of the process of natural selection. Such teleological explanations are both appropriate and inevitable in biology, yet remain fully compatible with standard causal accounts. They should not be

---

28. Darwin, *The Life and Letters of Charles Darwin*, 2:201.
29. Darwin, *The Life and Letters of Charles Darwin*, 2:201.
30. Mayr, "Teleological and Teleonomic," 104.
31. Ross, *Aristotle*, 74. Emphasis in original.
32. Ayala, "Teleological Explanations in Evolutionary Biology," 11.

reduced to non-teleological explanations, for they would then lose their explanatory power.

Although one cannot demonstratively prove the existence of God through reference to teleology, the congruence of such a position with the existence of God can be read from the interpretation of nature. In dialogue with McGrath, I posit that natural theology can be pictured as the process of "seeing" nature from the perspective of a Trinitarian ontology.[33] Christian theology provides an interpretative framework by which nature may be "seen" in a way that connects with the transcendent. The enterprise of natural theology would thus be one of discernment, of viewing it through a particular set of spectacles, as it were, which acknowledges nature as a legitimate, but limited, conduit to the divine reality.[34] This type of natural theology holds that nature reinforces an *existing* belief in God through the resonance between observation and theory. When properly understood, a renewed, defensible, natural theology represents a distinctively Christian way of viewing, beholding, envisaging, and appreciating the natural order—in ways that are not necessarily mandated by nature itself.

---

33. McGrath, *Darwinism and the Divine*, 201.
34. McGrath, *The Open Secret*, 3.

6

Conclusion

A New Natural Theology from Below—An Affirmation of Ontological Randomness and Purpose in Nature

In *The Structure of Evolutionary Theory*, Stephen Jay Gould emphasizes the importance of recognizing both the reality of structural constraint and the idea that structures have historical origins, which implies contingency. According to him, the history of life is not progressive, necessarily, and it is certainly not predictable. The earth's living systems have evolved through a series of unexpected, unplanned, and accidental events. Humans, for example, arose as a contingent outcome of thousands of linked events, any one of which could have occurred differently and thereby led evolutionary history on a pathway that possibly could not have led to the rise of consciousness. To mention just four examples among many:

1. If a member of our chordate phylum, *Pikaia*—which shows its relation to humans by its possession of a notochord—had not been among the survivors of the initial radiation of multicellular animal life in the Cambrian explosion circa 520 million years ago, then it is unlikely that vertebrates would have inhabited the earth at all;

Conclusion

2. If a small group of lobe-finned fishes had not evolved with a radically different limb skeleton, with a strong central axis perpendicular to the body, capable of bearing weight on land, then vertebrates possibly would never have become terrestrial;
3. If a meteorite had not struck the earth circa 65 million years ago, then dinosaurs would probably still be dominant today and mammals would still be small creatures living within the dinosaurs' world; and
4. If a small lineage of primates had not evolved upright posture on the African savannas just two million years ago, then our ancestry might have wound up as a line of ecologically marginal apes.[35]

We are indeed an item of evolutionary history and not an example of general principles within evolution.

In the introduction to this book, I argued that it is (still) possible to positively appraise God's activity and involvement within today's predominantly (or largely) secular evolutionary worldview. But some massaging of the details is needed. This introduction set up the argument to follow. In chapter 1, I argued for a tripartite contemporary relation of science and theology. In doing this, I arrived at a contemporary relation of science and theology, one that should be viewed as "overlapping," instead of separately viewed, as in the famous assertion of Stephen Jay Gould that science and religion should be in a state of respective non-interference of the other, that is, they should be "non-overlapping magesteria."[36] I then transitioned to an overview, in chapter 2, necessarily perspectival in orientation, of the secular evolutionary worldview (SEW). I covered major topics, theses, and sub-theses of this worldview, under the rubric of the roles of and for common ancestry, adaptation/ism, and selection/ism. Doing this enabled me (and the readers) to more deftly understand the worldview that is so oft set against any sort of theistic interpretation.

I then transitioned further, in chapter 3, into an exploration of what I termed "the God of chance." This third chapter is

---

35. Gould, *Wonderful Life*, 3.
36. Gould, "Non-overlapping Magisteria," 16–22.

Conclusion

critical to developing a new natural theology from below for the contemporary environ, I assert. Indeed, chance abounds in this (late-)modern world. In order, then, to have a proper understanding of the new natural theology from below that I assert herein, one must come to terms with the ever-pervasive chancy nature of the (late-)modern world. This probably constitutes the heart of the book, in my opinion, as I seek to highlight that even though chance is ever-pervasive throughout the uni-/multiverse, we cannot assure God's intentions may come to fruition, and even though chance runs counter to the intuited pattern of a life history influenced by a "loving God," God—the supreme architect of nature—can employ chance in achieving his purposes.

I showed this latter point in the next two chapters of the book, namely chapters 4 and 5. Indeed, in chapter 4, I explored a theological assist by the foremost theologian of science in the contemporary era, Philip Clayton (I say this not only because he is my mentor, but it is also indicatively true). Phil, as I affectionately call him, shows us that in relation to the God of contemporary science, the question of the divine agency has become one of the most difficult and urgent questions facing theologians today. Clayton also stipulates that the question is twofold: what resources can be found within theology—within the doctrines of God, nature, creation and redemption, for example—for addressing these well-known challenges? And what changes may be required in the traditional formulations of these doctrines in order to respond to those challenges that we find ourselves unable to solve?[37]

We saw that Clayton himself somewhat reflects the disposition of one of his own mentors, that is, Arthur R. Peacocke. For Peacocke, the problems with the details of a particular accounts suggest that theology is better off remaining at the level of *general* statements about God's purposes in the world. Peacocke himself once stated that the theologian may note the "new scientific awareness of unpredictability, open-endedness, and flexibility, and of the inbuilt propensities of natural processes to have particular kinds of

---

37. Clayton, *God and Contemporary Science*, 169.

Conclusion

outcomes."[38] But she should not go beyond these speakers of the world to try to specify the "causal joint" through which God brings about his purposes in the world.[39] According to Peacocke, then, we humans can never locate a locus of divine activity within the interstices of the world and then conceive of it being amplified to affect cosmic history. If God is to have any providential activity at all, the influence will move not from the part to the whole but from the whole to the part, which Peacocke calls "top-down" causation or "whole part constraint."[40]

Clayton's thesis, in short, is the following: the question of God's relation to the world, and hence the question of how to construe divine activity, "should be controlled by the best theories we have of the relationship of *our* minds to our bodies"—and then corrected for by the ways in which God's relation to the universe must be *different* from the relation of our mental properties to our brains and bodies.[41] Toward the end of *God and Contemporary Science*, Clayton gives the formulation of divine activity that I myself have carried forward into my dissertation,[42] as well as in the to-be-released book that corresponds to said dissertation.[43] Clayton writes, "One could argue that Spirit has been present in some way from the very beginning, somehow preceding humanity and even life itself, perhaps helping to bring about the higher life forms at the appropriate time. This would be a teleological view, since Spirit would be exercising a purpose in bringing about a goal from the very beginning."[44]

From the fifth chapter of this book, I assert that the enterprise of natural theology has, if anything, been given a new lease of life through the rise of evolutionary thought. The traditional approach to natural theology, aptly demonstrated by Aquinas and Paley, is

---

38. Peacocke, "Chance and Law," 143.

39. Clayton, *God and Contemporary Science*, 222.

40. Clayton, *God and Contemporary Science*, 222.

41. Clayton, *God and Contemporary Science*, 233.

42. McCall, "Contingency and Divine Activity."

43. McCall, *Macroevolution, Contingency, & Uncontrolling, Amorepotent Love*.

44. Clayton, *God and Contemporary Science*, 238–39.

Conclusion

merely one option among many; the rise of evolutionary thought supplemented an existing and vigorous theological critique of this approach. Natural theology needs to emerge from the shadows of this traditional approach and rediscover, retrieve, and renew alternative approaches. Natural theology cannot be understood to concern *proving* God from nature. Christians must do natural theology, rather, beholding the same realities as the general populace, and recast it as a process of "seeing" the domain of nature as affirming the resonance of what they observe with tenets of the Christian faith, without claiming that this observed resonance *proves* the truth of Christianity. After all, "the world at which the theologian looks and the world at which the secularist looks are one in the same."[45] This interpretive lens does not prove its truth; it does, however, demonstrate its utility, opening up in the process further areas of exploration and engagement.

In fact, it could be argued that Darwin's theory opened up new possibilities for natural theology, if we take the angle that it is through evolution that God makes his creation more complex. Indeed, as Charles Kingsley, a nineteenth-century Anglican divine noted, "We knew of old that God was so wise that he could make all things: but behold, he is so much wiser than even that, that he can make all things make themselves."[46] The perspective of the fifth chapter regarding natural theology, in sum, is that the posit of a renewed natural theology is about maximizing the intellectual "traction" between the Christian vision of reality and the observations of scientists.

Towards the end of chapter 3 of this text, I transitioned to a brief discussion of the influence that Charles Sanders Peirce has had upon the development of my own position. Although not fully broached in this book, I do intend in future years to write more about Peirce, for I find him most interesting and most perplexing at one and the same time. However, I will state now, in reference to Peirce, that his evolutionary developmental philosophy was not bounded by classical determinism, but he instead insisted that we

---

45. Smith, *The Free Man*, 45.
46. Kingsley, "The Natural Theology of the Future," xxvii.

Conclusion

must suppose an element of absolute chance, sporting, spontaneity, originality, and freedom in nature. In future publications, I will explicate three models of evolution that he advocated—comprised of tychism, anancasm, and agapism—which together provide a plausible account of evolution that is in some sense explainable by reference to teleology.[47]

Moreover, I will explain how Peirce, by virtue of his evolutionary developmental teleology, brought a unique understanding of reality to philosophy. Furthermore, in dialoguing with Peirce, I will draw from him a developmental teleological view, based upon the implicit arguments found within his seminal writings, which will then be applied to a rendition of teleology that may be palatable for the (late-)modern evolutionary sciences. The *telos* of this "evolutionary developmental teleology" will then be seen to be, broadly, increased complexity, a *telos* of which is ever growing. I will, moreover, note that Peirce interprets the interdependence of efficient and final causation as being one in which final causation without efficient causation is helpless, and efficient causation without final causation is worse than helpless—it is mere chaos.

A few further conclusions follow from this book. I suggest four things. First, there is genuine randomness in nature. God employs this randomness in order to achieve the maximal out-filling of creation by maintaining dynamic stability in complex systems. That is, God uses the inherent randomness of nature and thereafter employs it in a supervenient manner, to achieve his ends in the (uni-)multiverse. But second, this ontological randomness does not preclude the derivation of propensities toward the expression of similar form, even among widely divergent evolutionary lines. This concept is popularly referred to as "convergence" in the literature.

Third, the *God of chance* lavishes in arriving at the unexpected throughout the (macro-)evolutionary process. Therefore, fourth, we live in a world of both chance and purpose, which the philosophy of Peirce most excellently epitomizes. The evolutionary developmental teleology implicitly advocated by Peirce gives one the ability to maintain a methodologically *naturalistic* viewpoint

---

47. Cf. Bradford McCall, "The Erotic Creating Spirit."

Conclusion

but at the same time preserve objective divine involvement through the advocation a supernaturalistic *metaphysics*. Appropriating such for today means simply that theologians are to be methodological naturalists, but also metaphysical supernaturalists at the same time. For example, as a methodological naturalist, but also a metaphysical supernaturalist, I believe that that God worked with matter that was concurrent with him in the beginning, and that at the end of this natural world—whatever science ultimately decides the fate of it to be—God will bring to pass the second coming of the Christ, that is, the "anointed one," and instantiate whatever reality of heaven there is to come.

I would like now to offer a typology of sorts, for what the term "naturalism" generally has meant, does mean, and how patrons have appropriated it in the past and even today. Indeed, within his article in *The Oxford Handbook to Religion and Science*, Owen Flanagan notes fifteen different senses in which the term "naturalism" is used, ten of which I will note below, which have been modified by me:[48]

1. Philosophy should respect, be informed by, wholeheartedly accept, etc., the methods and claims of science.
2. When a well-grounded philosophical or theological claim and an equally well-grounded scientific claim clash, the scientific claim trumps the philosophical one.
3. Philosophical claims are not necessarily distinct from scientific ones, but differ, however, only in level of generality.
4. Science and theology, as well as philosophy for that matter, are only licensed to describe the way things actually are (i.e., realism) in the (uni-)multiverse.
5. Science and theology, as well as philosophy, are, moreover, concerned with giving naturalistic justifications for epistemic and ethical ideals and norms.
6. There is no need, or desire to need, the invocation of immaterial causes in describing the potentiation of things in this (uni-)multiverse.

---

48. Flanagan, "Varieties of Naturalism," 430–31.

Conclusion

7. Naturalism is another name for materialism in that it describes what is, what has been, and what shall be, as whatever fundamental physics ultimately decides them to be.
8. Naturalism is a thesis that itself rejects both physicalism and materialism inasmuch as there are natural but non-physical properties, as in informational states.
9. Naturalism claims that most knowledge is *a posteriori*.
10. Naturalism is foremost an epistemic thesis which explains why we should not make claims about everything there is.

The historical record shows that, as Darwin's ideas grew in influence, new ways of conceiving God, humanity, and the God-world relationship also began to be proposed. Like all other fields of human knowledge, theology had to—and still has to—have the humility to learn from Darwin. As Charles Kingsley, a distinctively nineteenth-century methodological naturalist[49] and Anglican priest, wrote to Darwin,

> I have gradually learnt to see that it is just as noble a conception of Deity, to believe that he created primal forms capable of self-development into all forms needful pro tempore and pro loco, as to believe that he required a fresh act of intervention to supply the lacunas which he himself had made. I question whether the former be not the loftier thought.[50]

This "loftier" theology *must* be a theology without literalism, without anthropomorphism, and without omnipotence, but with a God who involves himself as a cause alongside natural causes—that is, it must not offer a God who sets aside natural laws, but a God who works with and possibly within these regularities instead. What I mean by the invocation of that battery of terms is simply that as "humans" we should not view everything that happens in the natural world through a basically "human" lens. Further, God must not be seen to be "all-powerful" in the sense that he can do whatever he

---

49. Note that the "naturalism" of centuries previous to the twentieth and twenty-first was a remarkably different construct than the "naturalism" of today.

50. Kingsley, "Letter to Charles Darwin, 18 November 1859," 380.

Conclusion

wants, but instead as the chief enabler through the power of persuasion instead. So let me say plainly how I think theology should be done in the (Post-)Darwinian context. After Darwin, I suggest the following five proposals:

1. That theologians assume all objects in the natural world are composed of the same basic constituents that other things in this universe are composed of (hence no divinely imputed "soul," which is truly a neoplatonist idea, anyway).
2. That we assume that humans, like other animals, are natural objects with a natural history, not exceptions to the evolutionary process.
3. That we can no longer dichotomize between the realms of biology and culture, or between brain and mind. Culture is leashed to biology, sometimes by a short one and sometimes by a remarkably long one.
4. That theologians who study the natural world should be *methodological naturalists*, at least in the ways that made Darwin famous: collecting data, formulating theories and models to explain that data, and then looking for *natural* causes of the phenomena. And
5. That if there is a God, which I heartily do contend, God must be conceived as the source (in some manner) of the physical, chemical, and biological dynamics that exist in this universe; if one's notion of God does not allow for evolutionary history as it has actually unfolded, then that person's notion of God is definitely deficient, if not mistaken entirely.

Bibliography

Alston, William P. *Divine Nature and Human Language: Essays in Philosophical Theology*. Ithaca, New York: Cornell University Press, 1989.

Amundson, Ronald. "Doctor Dennett and Doctor Pangloss: Perfection and Selection in Psychology and Biology." *Behavioral and Brain Sciences* 13 (1990) 577–84.

———. "Logical Adaptationism." *Behavioral and Brain Sciences* 11 (1988) 505–06.

Aquinas, Thomas. *Summa Theologica*. Translated by The Fathers of the English Dominican Province. London: Burns, Oates, and Washbourne, 1911.

Aristotle. *Metaphysics*. Translated by H. Tredennick. 2 vols. Cambridge, Massachusetts: Harvard University Press, 1933.

———. *Parts of Animals. Movement of Animals. Progression of Animals*. Translated by A. L. Peck. Cambridge, Massachusetts: Harvard University Press, 1937.

———. *Physics*. Translated by P. H. Wicksteed and F. M. Cornford. 2 vols. Cambridge, Massachusetts: Harvard University Press, 1957.

Ayala, Francisco J. "Teleological Explanations in Evolutionary Biology." *Philosophy of Science* 37.1 (1970) 1–15.

Barbour, Ian G. *Religion in an Age of Science: The Gifford Lectures, Vol. 1: 1989-1991*. New York: Harper, 1991.

———. *When Science Meets Religion: Enemies, Strangers, or Partners?* New York: Harper, 2000.

Beatty, John H. "Chance and Design." In *The Cambridge Encyclopedia of Darwin and Evolutionary Thought*, edited by Michael Ruse, 146–51. Cambridge, UK: Cambridge University Press, 2013.

———. "Chance Variation: Darwin on Orchids." *Philosophy of Science* 73.5 (2006) 629–41.

———. "Replaying Life's Tape." *Journal of Philosophy* 103.7 (2006) 336–62.

Bibliography

Ben-Menahem, Yemima. "Historical Contingency." *Ratio* 10.2 (1997) 99–107.
———. "Historical Necessity and Contingency." In *A Companion to the Philosophy of History and Historiography*, edited by Aviezer Tucker, 120–30. Chichester, UK: Blackwell, 2009.
Blount, Zachary D. "History's Windings in a Flask: Microbial Experiments into Evolutionary Contingency." In *Chance in Evolution*, edited by Grant Ramsey and Charles Pence, 244–63. Chicago: University of Chicago Press, 2016.
Boorman, Scott A., and Paul R. Levitt. *The Genetics of Altruism*. New York: Academic, 1980.
Boyd, Robert, and Peter Richerson. *Culture and the Evolutionary Process*. Chicago: University of Chicago Press, 1985.
Brooke, John Hedley, and Geoffrey N. Cantor. *Reconstructing Nature: The Engagement of Science & Religion*. London: T. & T. Clark, 1998.
Brooke, John Hedley. *Science and Religion: Some Historical Perspectives*. Cambridge Studies in the History of Science. Cambridge, UK: Cambridge University Press, 1991.
Browning, Douglas, and William T. Myers. *Philosophers of Process*. New York: Fordham University Press, 1998.
Brümmer, Vincent, ed. *Interpreting the Universe as Creation*. Kampen, The Netherlands: The Kok Pharos Publishing House, 1991.
Brunner, Emil. "Natur und Gnade: Zum Gespräch mit Karl Barth." In *Ein offenes Wort. Voträge un Aufsätze*, edited by Rudolf Wehrli, 1917–34. Zürich: Theologischer Verlag, 1981.
Cain, A. J. "The Perfection of Animals." *Biological Journal of the Linnaean Society* 36 (1989) 3–29.
Carroll, Sean B. *Endless Forms Most Beautiful: The New Science of Evo Devo and the Making of the Animal Kingdom*. New York: Norton, 2005.
Cassidy, J. "Philosophical Aspects of the Group Selection Controversy." *British Journal for the Philosophy of Science* 45 (1978) 575–94.
Charnov, E. *The Theory of Sex Allocation*. Princeton, New Jersey: Princeton University Press, 1982.
Clayton, Philip. *God and Contemporary Science*. Edinburgh Studies in Constructive Theology. Grand Rapids, Michigan: Eerdmans, 1998.
———. "The Panentheistic Turn in Theology." *Dialog: A Journal of Theology* 38 (1999) 289–93.
Collier, Andrew. *Critical Realism: An Introduction to Roy Bhaskar's Philosophy*. London: Verso, 1994.
Collins English Dictionary. "Weltanschauung." https://www.collinsdictionary.com/us/dictionary/english/weltanschauung.
———. "Worldview." https://www.collinsdictionary.com/us/dictionary/english/worldview.
Conway Morris, Simon. *The Crucible of Creation: The Burgess Shale and the Rise of Animals*. Oxford, UK: Oxford University Press, 1998.

Bibliography

———. "Evolution: Like Any Other Science It Is Predictable." *Philosophical Transactions of the Royal Society of London* B 365.1537 (2010) 133–45.

———. *Life's Solution: Inevitable Humans in a Lonely Universe.* Cambridge, UK: Cambridge University Press, 2003.

———. "The Predictability of Evolution: Glimpses into a Post-Darwinian World." *Die Naturwissenschaften* 96.11 (2009) 1313–37.

Crick, Francis H. "The Origin of the Genetic Code." *Journal of Molecular Biology* 38.3 (1968) 367–79.

Darwin, Charles. *Autobiography.* http://darwin-online.org.uk/content/frameset?itemID=F1497&viewtype=text&pageseq=1.

———. *The Descent of Man and Selection in Relation to Sex.* 2 vols. New York: D. Appleton & Co., 1871–72.

———. *The Formation of Vegetable Mould, Through the Action of Worms.* London, UK: John Murray, 1881.

———. *Insectivorous Plants.* London, UK: John Murray, 1875.

———. "Letter 2814—C. R. Darwin to A. Gray, 22 May 1860." https://www.darwinproject.ac.uk/entry-2814.

———. "Letter 2998—C. R. Darwin to A. Gray, 26 Nov. 1860." https://www.darwinproject.ac.uk/entry-2998.

———. *On the Origin of Species by Means of Natural Selection; or the Preservation of Favoured Races in the Struggle for Life.* London, UK: John Murray, 1859.

———. *On the Origin of Species—A Variorum Edition.* Edited by M. Peckham. Philadelphia: University of Pennsylvania Press, 1959.

———. *On the Various Contrivances by which British and Foreign Orchids are Fertilised by Insects.* London, UK: John Murray, 1862.

Darwin, Charles, and Alfred Russel Wallace. "On the Tendency of Species to Form Varieties; and on the Perpetuation of Varieties and Species by Natural Means of Selection." *Proceedings of the Linnean Society, Zoological Journal* 3 (1858) 46–62.

Darwin, Erasmus. *The Temple of Nature.* London, UK: J. Johnson, 1803.

———. *Zoonomia: Or the Laws of Organic Life.* Philadelphia: Edward Earle, 1794.

Darwin, Francis, ed. *The Life and Letters of Charles Darwin.* 3 vols. London, UK: John Murray, 1887.

Davies, Nicholas B., and John R. Krebs. *An Introduction to Behavioral Ecology.* Sunderland, Massachusetts: Sinauer, 1981.

Dawkins, Richard. *The Extended Phenotype.* Oxford, UK: Oxford University Press, 1982.

———. *The Selfish Gene.* Oxford, UK: Oxford University Press, 1976.

de La Mettrie, J. O. "L'homme machine." In *Oeuvres philosophiques.* Amsterdam, The Netherlands, 1764.

de Maupertuis, P. L. M. "Essai de cosmologie." In *Oeuvres*, 1:1–58. Lyon, France: J. M. Bruyset, 1752.

Dennett, Daniel. C. *Darwin's Dangerous Idea.* New York: Simon & Schuster, 1995.

Bibliography

Depew, David J., and Bruce H. Weber, eds. *Evolution at a Crossroads: The New Biology and the New Philosophy of Science*. Cambridge, Massachusetts: The MIT Press, 1985.

Depew, David J. "Accident, Adaptation, and Teleology in Aristotle and Darwinism." In *Darwin in the Twenty-First Century: Nature, Humanity, God*, edited by Phillip R. Sloan, Gerald McKenny, and Kathleen Eggleston, 116–43. Notre Dame, Indiana: Notre Dame University Press, 2015.

———. "Contingency, Chance, and Randomness in Ancient, Medieval, and Modern Biology." In *Chance in Evolution*, edited by Grant Ramsey and Charles Pence, 15–40. Chicago: University of Chicago Press, 2016.

———. "Incidentally Final Causation and Spontaneous Generation in Aristotle's Physics II and Other Texts." In *Was ist Leben? Aristoteles' Anschauungen zur Entstehung und Funktionsweise von Leben*, edited by Sabine Föllinger, 285–97. Stuttgart, Germany: Franz Steiner Verlag, 2010.

Dobzhansky, Theodosius. *The Biological Basis of Human Freedom*. New York: Columbia University Press, 1956.

———. *The Biology of Ultimate Concern*. New York: New American Library, 1967.

———. *Genetics and the Origin of Species*. New York: Columbia University Press, 1937.

———. *Mankind Evolving: The Evolution of the Human Species*. New Haven, Connecticut: Yale University Press, 1962.

———. "Nothing in Biology Makes Sense Except in the Light of Evolution." *American Biology Teacher* 35 (1973) 125–29.

Dobzhansky, Theodosius, and Ernest Boesiger. *Human Culture: A Moment in Evolution*. New York: Columbia University Press, 1987.

Eaton, T. H. "The Aquatic Origin of Tetrapods." *Transactions of the Kansas Academy of Science* 63 (1960) 115–20.

Edwards, Denis. *How God Acts: Creation, Redemption, and Special Divine Action*. Minneapolis: Fortress, 2010.

Edwards, J. L. "Two Perspectives on the Evolution of the Tetrapod Limb." *American Zoologist* 29 (1989) 235–54.

Erwin, Douglas H. "*Wonderful Life* Revisited: Chance and Contingency in the Ediacaran-Cambrian Radiation." In *Chance in Evolution*, edited by Grant Ramsey and Charles Pence, 277–98. Chicago: University of Chicago Press, 2016.

Feser, Edward. *Aquinas: A Beginner's Guide*. Beginner's Guides. London, UK: Oneworld, 2009.

Fisher, Ronald A. *The Genetical Theory of Natural Selection*. Oxford, UK: Clarendon, 1930.

———. "Indeterminism and Natural Selection." *Philosophy of Science* 1.1 (1934) 99–117.

Flanagan, Owen. "Varieties of Naturalism." In *The Oxford Handbook to Religion and Science*, edited by Philip Clayton and Zachary Simpson, 430–31. Oxford, UK: Oxford University Press, 2008.

Bibliography

Francis, Pope. *The Joy of the Gospel: Evangelii Gaudium*. Culver City, California: Pauline Books & Media, 2014.

Freud, Sigmund. *New Introductory Lectures in Psycho-Analysis*. Edited by James Strachey. New York: W. W. Norton, 1990.

Gardner, A., and A. Grafen. "Capturing the Superorganism—A Formal Theory of Group Adaptation." *Journal of Evolutionary Biology* 22 (2009) 659–71.

Gasper, P. "An Interview with Philip Kitcher." *Human Nature Review* 4 (2004) 82–89.

Gayon, Jean. "Chance, Explanation, and Causation in Evolutionary Theory." *History and Philosophy of the Life Sciences* 27.3/4 (2005) 395–405.

———. *Darwinism's Struggle for Survival: Heredity and the Hypothesis of Natural Selection*. Cambridge, UK: Cambridge University Press, 1998.

Ghiselin, Michael T. *The Triumph of the Darwinian Method*. Berkeley, California: University of California Press, 1969.

Gigerenzer, Gerd, et al. *The Empire of Chance: How Probability Changed Science and Everyday Life*. Cambridge, UK: Cambridge University Press, 1989.

Godfrey-Smith, Peter. "Three Kinds of Adaptationism." In *Adaptationism and Optimality*, edited by Steven H. Orzack and Elliott Sober, 335–57. New York: Cambridge University Press, 2001.

Gould, Stephen Jay, and Richard C. Lewontin. "The Spandrels of San Marco and the Panglossian Paradigm: A Critique of the Adaptationist Programme." *Proceedings of the Royal Society of London* B.205 (1979) 581–98.

Gould, Stephen Jay. "The Hardening of the Modern Synthesis." In *Dimensions of Darwinism*, edited by Marjorie Grene, 71–93. Cambridge, UK: Cambridge University Press, 1983.

———. "Non-overlapping Magisteria." *Natural History* 106.3 (1997) 16–22.

———. *Rocks of Ages: Science and Religion in the Fullness of Life*. New York: Ballantine, 1999.

———. *The Structure of Evolutionary Theory*. Cambridge, Massachusetts: Harvard University Press, 2002.

———. *Wonderful Life: The Burgess Shale and the Nature of History*. New York: W. W. Norton & Co., 1989.

Graham, Loren R. *Between Science and Values*. New York: Columbia University Press, 1984.

Gray, Asa. *Darwiniana: Essays and Reviews Pertaining to Darwinism*. New York: Appleton, 1884.

Griffin, David Ray. *Unsnarling the World-Knot: Consciousness, Freedom, and the Mind-Body Problem*. Eugene, Oregon: Wipf & Stock, 2008.

Griffiths, Peter E. "In What Sense Does 'Nothing Make Sense Except in the Light of Evolution'?" *Acta Biotheoretica* 57 (2009) 11–32.

Hacking, Ian. *The Taming of Chance*. Cambridge, UK: Cambridge University Press, 1990.

Haldane, J. B. S. *New Paths in Genetics*. New York: Harper, 1942.

Harris, C. Leon. *Evolution: Genesis and Revelations, with Readings from Empedocles to Wilson*. Albany, New York: State University Press of New York, 1981.

Bibliography

Hartshorne, Charles. *Creativity in American Philosophy*. Albany, New York: State University of New York Press, 1984.

———. *The Logic of Perfection and Other Essays in Neoclassical Metaphysics*. Whitefish, Montana: Literary Licensing, 2011.

———. *Man's Vision of God and the Logic of Theism*. Chicago: Willett, Clark, & Co., 1941.

Hartl, Daniel L., and Andrew G. Clark. *Principles of Population Genetics*. Sunderland, Massachusetts: Sinauer, 1980.

Harvey, Paul H., and Mark D. Pagel. *The Comparative Method in Evolutionary Biology*. Oxford, UK: Oxford University Press, 1991.

Haught, John F. *Making Sense of Evolution: Darwin, God, and the Drama of Life*. Louisville, Kentucky: Westminster John Knox, 2010.

———. *The New Cosmic Story: Inside Our Awakening Universe*. New Haven, Connecticut: Yale University Press, 2017.

———. *Resting on the Future: Catholic Theology for an Unfinished Universe*. New York: Bloomsbury, 2015.

Hauerwas, Stanley. *With the Grain of the Universe: The Church's Witness and Natural Theology*. Ada, Michigan: Brazos, 2001.

Hodge, Jonathon. "Chance and Chances in Darwin's Early Theorizing and in Darwinian Theory Today." In *Chance in Evolution*, edited by Grant Ramsey and Charles Pence, 41–75. Chicago: University of Chicago Press, 2016.

Hodge, M. J. S., and Gregory Radick. "The Place of Darwin's Theories in the Intellectual Long Run." In *The Cambridge Companion to Darwin*, edited by M. J. S. Hodge and Gregory Radick, 246–73. 2nd ed. Cambridge, UK: Cambridge University Press, 2009.

Hookway, Christopher. "Design and Chance: The Evolution of Peirce's Evolutionary Cosmology." In *Truth, Rationality, and Pragmatism: Themes from Peirce*, edited by Christopher Hookway, 159–81. Oxford, UK: Oxford University Press, 2000.

Hume, David. *An Enquiry Concerning Human Understanding*. London: A. Millar, 1748.

Huxley, Julian. *At Random*. Aired November 21, 1959.

———. *Evolution: The Modern Synthesis*. London: Allen and Unwin, 1942.

Huxley, Thomas H. *Lay Sermons, Addresses, and Reviews*. London: Macmillan, 1870.

Inkpen, Rob, and Derek D. Turner. "The Topography of Historical Contingency." *Journal of the Philosophy of History* 6.1 (2012) 1–19.

Jackson, F., and P. Pettit. "In Defense of Explanatory Ecumenism." *Economics and Philosophy* 8 (1992) 1–22.

Kim, Jaegwon. "Downward Causation." In *Emergence or Reduction?: Essays on the Prospects of Non-reductive Physicalism*, edited by Ansgar Beckermann et al., 119–38. Berlin: Walter de Gruyter, 1992.

Kimura, Motoo. *The Neutral Theory of Molecular Evolution*. Cambridge, UK: Cambridge University Press, 1983.

Bibliography

Kingsley, Charles. "Letter to Charles Darwin, 18 November 1859." In *The Correspondence of Charles Darwin, Vol. 7: 1858-1859*, edited by Fredrick Burkhardt et al., 380-82. Cambridge, UK: Cambridge University Press, 1992.

———. "The Natural Theology of the Future. Delivered at Sion College, London, 10 January 1871." In *Scientific Lectures and Essays*, 329-30. London: Macmillan, 1893.

Kitcher, Philip, et al. "The Illusory Riches of Sober's Monism." *Journal of Philosophy* 87 (1990) 158-61.

Kitcher, Philip. *The Advancement of Science: Science without Legend, Objectivity without Illusions*. Oxford, UK: Oxford University Press, 1995.

Koonin, Eugene V. "Comparative Genomics, Minimal Gene-sets, and the Last Universal Common Ancestor." *Nature Reviews Microbiology* 1 (2003) 127-36.

Krüger, Lorenz, et al., eds. *The Probabilistic Revolution, Vol. 1: Ideas in History*. Cambridge, Massachusetts: Bradford, 1987.

———, eds. *The Probabilistic Revolution, Vol. 2: Ideas in the Sciences*. Cambridge, Massachusetts: Bradford, 1987.

Kuhn, Thomas. *The Structure of Scientific Revolutions*. Chicago: University of Chicago Press, 1962.

Kurtz, Paul, ed. *The Humanist Alternative*. Buffalo, New York: Prometheus, 1973.

Landsman, Klaas, et al. "Introduction." In *The Challenge of Chance: A Multidisciplinary Approach from the Sciences and the Humanities*, edited by Klaas Landsman and Ellen van Wolde, 1-7. Zürich: Springer Open, 2016.

Landsman, Klaas, and Ellen van Wolde, eds. *The Challenge of Chance: A Multidisciplinary Approach from the Sciences and the Humanities*. Zürich: Springer Open, 2016.

Lennox, James G. *Aristotle's Philosophy of Biology*. Cambridge, UK: Cambridge University Press, 2000.

———. "Darwin and Teleology." In The *Cambridge Encyclopedia of Darwin and Evolutionary Thought*, edited by Michael Ruse, 152-57. Cambridge, UK: Cambridge University Press, 2013.

———. "Darwin *Was* a Teleologist." *Biology & Philosophy* 8 (1993) 409-21.

———. "The Darwin/Gray Correspondence 1857-1869: An Intelligent Discussion about Chance and Design." *Perspectives on Science* 18.4 (2010) 456-79.

———. "Teleology by Another Name: A Reply to Ghiselin." *Biology & Philosophy* 9 (1994) 493-95.

Lewin, Roger. "Evolutionary Theory Under Fire." *Science* 210 (1980) 883-87.

Lewis, C. S. *Poems*. Edited by W. Hooper. London: Harcourt, 1964.

Lewontin, Richard C., Steven Rose, and Leon J. Kamin. *Not in Our Genes: Biology, Ideology, and Human Nature*. New York: Pantheon, 1984.

Lüthy, Christoph H., and Carla Rita Palmerino. "Conceptual and Historical Reflections on Chance (and Related Concepts)." In *The Challenge of Chance:*

Bibliography

A Multidisciplinary Approach from the Sciences and the Humanities, edited by Klaas Landsman and Ellen van Wolde, 9–47. Zürich: Springer Open, 2016.

May, Robert M., ed. *Theoretical Ecology: Principles and Applications*. 2nd ed. Sunderland, Massachusetts: Sinauer, 1981.

Mayr, Ernst. "Biology in the Twenty-First Century." *Bioscience* 50 (2000) 895–97.

———. *The Growth of Biological Thought*. Cambridge, Massachusetts: Harvard University Press, 1982.

———. "How to Carry Out the Adaptationist Program?" *The American Naturalist* 121 (1983) 324–34.

———. *Systematics and the Origin of Species from the Viewpoint of a Zoologist*. New York: Columbia University Press, 1942.

———. "Teleological and Teleonomic: A New Analysis." *Boston Studies in the Philosophy of Science* 14 (1974) 91–117.

———. *Towards a New Philosophy of Biology*. Cambridge, Massachusetts: Harvard University Press, 1988.

———. "Typological versus Population Thinking." In *Evolution and the Diversity of Life: Selected Essays*, 26–29. Cambridge, Massachusetts: Belknap, 1976.

McCall, Bradford. "Aquinas, Teleology, and the Modern Evolutionary Synthesis." *Man In Culture* 26 (2016) 375–95.

———. "Contingency and Divine Activity: Toward A Contemporary Conception of Divine Involvement in an Evolutionary World." PhD diss, Claremont School of Theology, 2021.

———. "Emergence and Kenosis: A Theological Synthesis." *Zygon: Journal of Science and Religion* 45.1 (2010) 149–64.

———. "The Erotic Creating Spirit: How Erotic Love Characterizes the Spirit of Creativity." Unpublished manuscript.

———. *Evolution: Secular or Sacred?* Eugene, Oregon: Wipf & Stock, 2020.

———. "Evolution, Emergence, and Final Causality: A Proposed Pneumatico-Theological Synthesis." *Wesleyan Theological Journal* 52.2 (2017) 148–64.

———, ed. *God and Gravity: A Philip Clayton Reader on Science and Theology*. Eugene, Oregon: Cascade, 2018.

———. *Macroevolution, Contingency, & Uncontrolling, Amorepotent Love: How God Works in the (Late-)Modern World*. Eugene, Oregon: Pickwick, forthcoming, 2022.

———. *A Modern Relation of Theology and Science Assisted by Emergence and Kenosis*. Eugene, Oregon: Wipf & Stock, 2018.

———, ed. *The Peacocke's Tale: An Arthur R. Peacocke Reader on Science & Faith*. Eugene, Oregon: Wipf & Stock, forthcoming, 2023.

———, ed. *Reading Ruse: Michael Ruse on Darwinism, Science, & Faith*. Eugene, Oregon: Pickwick, forthcoming, 2022.

McGhee, George R. *Convergent Evolution: Endless Forms Most Beautiful*. Cambridge, Massachusetts: The MIT Press, 2011.

Bibliography

McGrath, Alister E. *Darwinism and the Divine: Evolutionary Thought and Natural Theology*. Hoboken, New Jersey: Wiley-Blackwell, 2011.

———. *A Fine-Tuned Universe: The Quest for God in Science and Theology*. The Gifford Lectures. Louisville, Kentucky: Westminster John Knox, 2009.

———. *The Open Secret: A New Vision for Natural Theology*. West Sussex, UK: Wiley-Blackwell, 2008.

———. *A Scientific Theology, Vol. 2: Reality*. London: T. & T. Clark International, 2011.

Mitchell, W., and T. Valone. "The Optimization Research Program: Studying Adaptations by Their Function." *Quarterly Review of Biology* 65 (1990) 43–52.

Moltmann, Jürgen. *God in Creation: A New Theology of Creation and the Spirit of God*. Minneapolis: Fortress, 1993.

Moore, James. "Darwin's Progress and the Problem of Slavery." *Progress in Human Geography* 34.5 (2010) 555–82.

Murdoch, Iris. *Metaphysics as a Guide to Morals*. London: Penguin, 1994.

———. *The Sovereignty of Good*. Routledge Great Minds. Oxford, UK: Routledge, 2013.

Orzack, Seven H., and Elliot Sober. *Adaptation and Optimality*. Cambridge, UK: Cambridge University Press, 2000.

———. "Optimality Models and the Test of Adaptationism." *American Naturalist* 143 (1994) 361–80.

Ospovat, Dov. *The Development of Darwin's Theory: Natural History, Natural Theology, and Natural Selection 1838–1859*. Cambridge, UK: Cambridge University Press, 1981.

Oster, George F., and Edward O. Wilson. *Caste and Ecology in the Social Insects*. Princeton, New Jersey: Princeton University Press, 1978.

Parker, G., and John Maynard Smith. "Optimality Theory in Evolutionary Biology." *Nature* 348 (1990) 27–33.

Peacocke, Arthur R. "Chance and Law in Irreversible Thermodynamics, Theoretical Biology, and Theology." In *Chaos and Complexity: Scientific Perspectives on Divine Action*, edited by Robert Russell et al., 123–46. Vatican: Vatican Observatory, 1996.

Peirce, C. S. "The Doctrine of Necessity Examined." *The Monist* 2 (1892) 321–37.

———. "Evolutionary Love." *The Monist* 3.2 (1893) 176–200.

Pence, Charles. "The Early History of Chance in Evolution." *Studies in History and Philosophy of Science* 50 (2015) 48–58.

Plantinga, Alvin. "Science: Augustinian or Duhemian?" *Ratio* 19.4 (2006) 495–504.

Plutynski, Anya, et al. "Chance in the Modern Synthesis." In *Chance in Evolution*, edited by Grant Ramsey and Charles Pence, 76–102. Chicago: University of Chicago Press, 2016.

Porter, Theodore M. *The Rise of Statistical Thinking, 1820–1900*. Princeton, New Jersey: Princeton University Press, 1986.

Bibliography

Provine, William B. *Sewall Wright and Evolutionary Biology*. Chicago: University of Chicago Press, 1986.

Quetelet, Adolphe. *Sur l'homme et le développement de ses facultés, ou Essai de physique sociale*. 2 vols. Paris: Bachelier, 1835.

Ramsey, Grant, and Charles H. Pence, eds. *Chance in Evolution*. Chicago: University of Chicago Press, 2016.

———. "Chance in Evolution from Darwin to Contemporary Biology." In *Chance in Evolution*, edited by Grant Ramsey and Charles Pence, 1–11. Chicago: University of Chicago Press, 2016.

Raup, David M., and J. W. Valentine. "Multiple Origins of Life." *Proceedings of the Natural Academy of Sciences, USA* 80 (1983) 2981–84.

Richards, Robert J. *Darwin and the Emergence of Evolutionary Theories of Mind and Behavior*. Chicago: University of Chicago Press, 1987.

———. *The Meaning of Evolution: The Morphological Construction and Ideological Reconstruction of Darwin's Theory*. Chicago: University of Chicago Press, 1992.

Ridley, Matt. *The Explanation of Organic Diversity*. Oxford, UK: Oxford University Press, 1983.

Rose, Michael R., and George V. Lauder. *Adaptation*. Cambridge, UK: Cambridge Academic, 1996.

Ross, W. D. *Aristotle*. London: Methuen & Co., 1949.

Roughgarden, Jan. *Theory of Population Genetics and Evolutionary Ecology: An Introduction*. New York: Macmillan, 1979.

Ruse, Michael, and Edward O. Wilson. "Moral Philosophy as Applied Science." In *Conceptual Issues in Evolutionary Biology*, edited by Elliot Sober, 555–74. 3rd ed. Cambridge, Massachusetts: The MIT Press, 2006.

Ruse, Michael. *Darwin and Design*. Cambridge, Massachusetts: Harvard University Press, 2003.

———. "Does Darwinian Evolution Mean We Are Here by Chance?" In *Chance in Evolution*, edited by Grant Ramsey and Charles Pence, 122–42. Chicago: University of Chicago Press, 2016.

———. *Evolutionary Naturalism: Selected Essays*. Oxford, UK: Routledge, 1995.

———. "How Evolution Became a Religion." *National Post*, May 13, 2000.

———. *Monad to Man: The Concept of Progress in Evolutionary Biology*. Cambridge, Massachusetts: Harvard University Press, 1996.

Russell, Bertrand. "On the Notion of Cause." *Proceedings of the Aristotelian Society* 13 (1913) 1–26.

Russett, Cynthia Eagle. *Darwin in America: The Intellectual Response, 1865–1912*. New York: W. H. Freeman & Co., 1976.

Sagan, Carl. *Cosmos*. New York: Random House, 1980.

Schrödinger, Erwin. *Expanding Universes*. Cambridge, UK: Cambridge University Press, 1956.

Sebright, J. *The Art of Improving the Breeds of Domestic Animals in a Letter Addressed to the Right Hon. Sir Joseph Banks, K. B.* London, 1809.

Bibliography

Shipway, Brad. "The Theological Application of Bhaskar's Stratified Reality: The Scientific Theology of A. E. McGrath." *Journal of Critical Realism* 3.1 (2004) 191–203.

Simpson, George Gaylord. *The Meaning of Evolution*. New Haven, Connecticut: Yale University Press, 1971.

———. *Tempo and Mode in Evolution*. New York: Columbia University Press, 1944.

Sire, James W. *Discipleship of the Mind*. Downers Grove, Illinois: Intervarsity, 1990.

Sloan, Philip R., and Brandon Fogel. *Creating a Physical Biology: The Three-Man Paper and Early Molecular Biology*. Chicago: University of Chicago Press, 2011.

Sleeper, R. W. *The Necessity of Pragmatism: John Dewey's Conception of Philosophy*. Champaign, Illinois: University of Illinois Press, 2001.

Smith, John Maynard. *Evolution and the Theory of Games*. Cambridge, UK: Cambridge University Press, 1982.

———. "Group Selection and Kin Selection." *Nature* 201 (1964) 1145–46.

———. "How to Model Evolution." In *The Latest on the Best: Essays on Evolution and Optimality*, edited by J. Dupre, 117–31. Cambridge, Massachusetts: The MIT Press, 1987.

———. "Optimization Theory in Evolution." *Annual Review of Ecology and Systematics* 9 (1978) 31–56.

Smith, Ronald Gregor. *The Free Man: Studies in Christian Anthropology*. New York: HarperCollins, 1969.

Sober, Elliott. *Did Darwin Write the Origin Backwards? Philosophical Essays on Darwin's Theory*. Amherst, New York: Prometheus, 2011.

———. "Did Darwin Write the Origin Backwards?" *Proceedings of the National Academy of Sciences* 106 (2009) 10,048–55.

———. *Evidence & Evolution: The Logic Behind the Science*. Cambridge, UK: Cambridge University Press, 2008.

———. "Evolution and Optimality: Feathers, Bowling Balls, and the Thesis of Adaptationism." *Philosophic Exchange* 26 (1996) 41–55.

———. "The Multiple Realizability Argument against Reductionism." *Philosophy of Science* 66 (1999) 542–64.

———. *The Nature of Selection*. Cambridge, Massachusetts: The MIT Press, 1984.

———. *Philosophy of Biology*. Boulder, Colorado: Westview, 2000.

———. "Three Differences Between Evolution and Deliberation." In *Modeling Rationality, Morality, and Evolution*, edited by Peter A. Danielson, 408–22. Oxford, UK: Oxford University Press, 1998.

Sober, Elliott, and Mike Steel. "Testing the Hypothesis of Common Ancestry." *Journal of Theoretical Biology* 218 (2002) 395–408.

Sober, Elliott, and David Sloan Wilson. *Unto Others: The Evolution and Psychology of Unselfish Behavior*. Cambridge, Massachusetts: Harvard University Press, 1998.

Bibliography

Stebbins, G. Ledyard. *Variation and Evolution in Plants*. New York: Columbia University Press, 1950.

Steel, Mike, and Penny David. "Origins of Life: Common Ancestry Put to the Test." *Nature* 465 (2010) 168-69.

Stenmark, Mikael. *How to Relate Science and Religion: A Multidimensional Model*. Grand Rapids, Michigan: Eerdmans, 2004.

Sterelny, Kim, and Paul Griffiths. *Sex and Death*. Chicago: University of Chicago Press, 1999.

Sterelny, Kim, and Philip Kitcher. "The Return of the Gene." *Journal of Philosophy* 85 (1988) 339-60.

Tax, Sol, ed. *Evolution After Darwin, Vol. 1: The Evolution of Life*. Chicago: University of Chicago Press, 1960.

Theobald, Douglas L. "A Formal Test of the Theory of Universal Common Ancestry." *Nature* 465 (2010) 219-22.

Travisano, Michael, et al. "Experimental Tests of the Roles of Adaptation, Chance, and History in Evolution." *Science* 267 (1995) 87-90.

Turner, Derek D. "Gould's Replay Revisited." *Biology & Philosophy* 26.1 (2011) 65-79.

van Huyssteen, Wentzel. *Duet or Duel?: Theology and Science in a Postmodern World*. London: SCM, 1998.

Voltaire. *Collection Complete Des Oeuvres de Mr. de Voltaire, Vol. 5: Mélanges de Philosophie*. London, 1772.

Wagner, Gunter P., et al. "Developmental Evolution as a Mechanistic Science: The Inference from Developmental Mechanisms to Evolutionary Processes." *American Zoologist* 40 (2000) 819-31.

Waters, C. K. "Tempered Realism about Units of Selection." *Philosophy of Science* 58 (1991) 553-73.

———. "Why Genic and Multilevel Selection Theories Are Here to Stay." *Philosophy of Science* 72 (2005) 311-33.

Weiss, Madeline C., et al. "The Physiology and Habitat of the Last Universal Common Ancestor." *Nature Microbiology* 1.9 (2016) 16,116.

West-Eberhard, Mary J. *Developmental Plasticity and Evolution*. New York: Oxford University Press, 2003.

West, S., A. Griffin, and A. Gardner. "Social Semantics: Altruism, Cooperation, Mutualism, Strong Reciprocity, and Group Selection." *Journal of Evolutionary Biology* 20 (2009) 415-32.

Whitehead, Alfred North. *Adventures of Ideas*. New York: Free Press, 1933.

———. *Process and Reality: The Gifford Lectures, 1927-28*. New York: Free Press, 1979.

Wild, G., et al. "Adaptation and the Evolution of Parasite Virulence in a Connected World." *Nature* 459 (2009) 983-86.

Wilkins, John S. *Species: A History of the Idea*. Berkeley, California: University of California Press, 2009.

Bibliography

Williams, George. *Adaptation and Natural Selection: A Critique of Some Current Evolutionary Thought*. Princeton, New Jersey: Princeton University Press, 2018.

Wilson, David Sloan. "Levels of Selection: An Alternative to Individualism in Biology and the Human Sciences." In *Conceptual Issues in Evolutionary Biology*, edited by Elliot Sober, 63–78. 3rd ed. Cambridge, Massachusetts: The MIT Press, 2006.

———. *The Natural Selection of Populations and Communities*. Menlo Park, California: Benjamin/Cummings, 1980.

Wilson, Edward O. *Sociobiology: The New Synthesis*. Cambridge, Massachusetts: Belknap, 1975.

Williams, George C. "A Defense of Reductionism in Evolutionary Biology." In *Oxford Surveys in Evolutionary Biology*, edited by Richard Dawkins and Matt Ridley, 1–27. Oxford, UK: Oxford University Press, 1985.

Woese, Carl, et al. "Towards a Natural System of Organisms: Proposal for the Domains of Archaea, Bacteria, and Eukaraya." *Proceedings of the National Academy of Sciences, USA* 87.12 (1990) 4576–79.

Wright, Sewall. "Evolution in Mendelian Populations." *Genetics* 16.2 (1931) 97–159.

———. "The Roles of Mutation, Inbreeding, Crossbreeding, and Selection in Evolution." *Proceedings of the Sixth International Congress of Genetics* 1 (1932) 356–66.

Young, Robert M. *Darwin's Metaphor: Nature's Place in Victorian Culture*. Cambridge, UK: Cambridge University Press, 1985.

www.ingramcontent.com/pod-product-compliance
Lightning Source LLC
Chambersburg PA
CBHW070911160426
43193CB00011B/1428